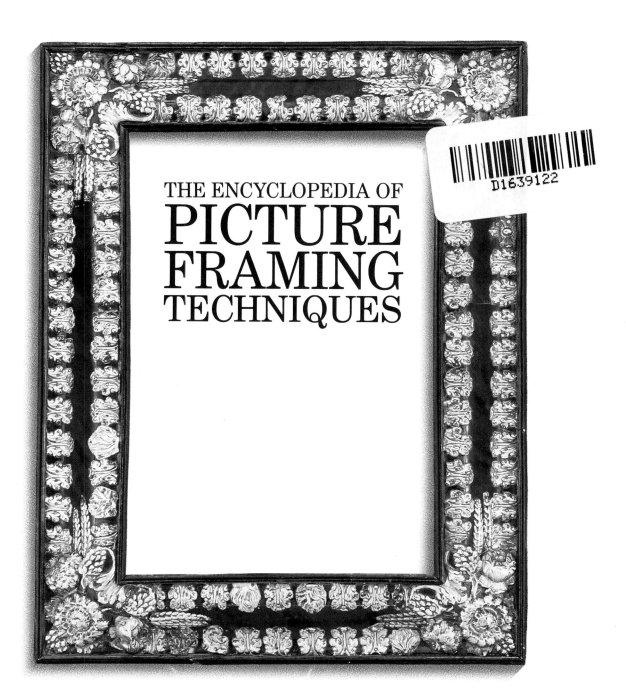

THE ENCYCLOPEDIA OF
PICTURE
FRAMING
TECHNIQUES

This pedimented frame with a marble finish (above) is a modern version of a traditional type. An attractive frame (right) with a lapis lazuli finish. Both pieces were made by Robert Cunning.

THE ENCYCLOPEDIA OF
PICTURE
FRAMING
TECHNIQUES

ROBERT CUNNING

SEARCH PRESS

A QUARTO BOOK

First published in Great Britain in paperback 2002 by

Search Press Ltd
Wellwood
North Farm Road
Tunbridge Wells
Kent TN2 3DR

ISBN 1 903975 28 X

This book was designed and produced by

Quarto Publishing plc
The Old Brewery
6, Blundell Street
London N7 9BH

Senior Editor Hazel Harrison
Art Editor Penny Cobb
Designer Terry Jeavons
Photographers Paul Forrester, Ian Howes and Chas
Wilder
Picture Researcher Amanda Little
Diagrams Ed Stuart
Art director Moira Clinch
Publishing Director Janet Slingsby

Typeset in Tunbridge Wells by En to En
Manufactured by Eray Scan, Singapore
Printed in China by Leefung Asco. Printers Ltd

A delicate paint finish with subtle
touches of gold on the ornament and
inner edge complements the gentle
colours of the floral print. The frame
was made by Patrick Ireland.

CONTENTS

CHAPTER 7
GILDING

CHAPTER 8
RESTORATION
AND REPAIR

CHAPTER 9
A GALLERY OF
FRAMES

PUBLISHER'S NOTE

Working with paints and varnishes demands care, as some of the mineral pigments used in paints are poisonous, and the solvents are highly toxic. Always follow the manufacturer's instructions regarding safety, and store chemicals and other toxic substances well out of reach of children. Neither the author, copyright holder or publisher can accept any liability for accidents.

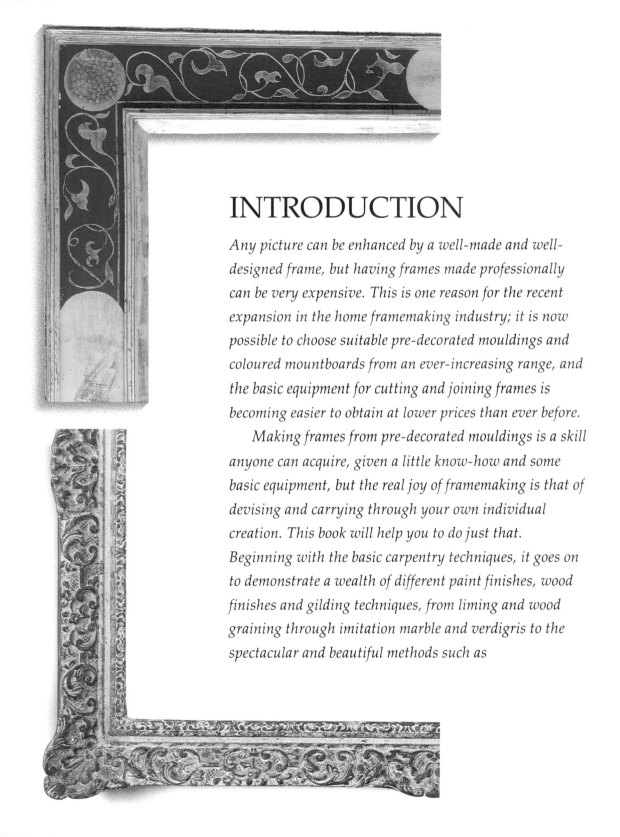

INTRODUCTION

Any picture can be enhanced by a well-made and well-designed frame, but having frames made professionally can be very expensive. This is one reason for the recent expansion in the home framemaking industry; it is now possible to choose suitable pre-decorated mouldings and coloured mountboards from an ever-increasing range, and the basic equipment for cutting and joining frames is becoming easier to obtain at lower prices than ever before.

Making frames from pre-decorated mouldings is a skill anyone can acquire, given a little know-how and some basic equipment, but the real joy of framemaking is that of devising and carrying through your own individual creation. This book will help you to do just that. Beginning with the basic carpentry techniques, it goes on to demonstrate a wealth of different paint finishes, wood finishes and gilding techniques, from liming and wood graining through imitation marble and verdigris to the spectacular and beautiful methods such as

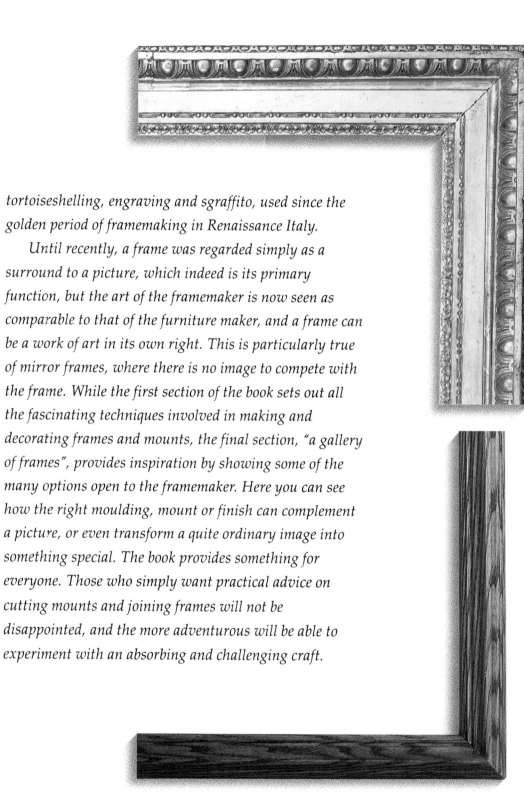

tortoiseshelling, engraving and sgraffito, used since the golden period of framemaking in Renaissance Italy.

    Until recently, a frame was regarded simply as a surround to a picture, which indeed is its primary function, but the art of the framemaker is now seen as comparable to that of the furniture maker, and a frame can be a work of art in its own right. This is particularly true of mirror frames, where there is no image to compete with the frame. While the first section of the book sets out all the fascinating techniques involved in making and decorating frames and mounts, the final section, "a gallery of frames", provides inspiration by showing some of the many options open to the framemaker. Here you can see how the right moulding, mount or finish can complement a picture, or even transform a quite ordinary image into something special. The book provides something for everyone. Those who simply want practical advice on cutting mounts and joining frames will not be disappointed, and the more adventurous will be able to experiment with an absorbing and challenging craft.

CHAPTER 1

MATERIALS AND EQUIPMENT

Few people have large, well equipped workshops at their disposal; the majority of us have to be satisfied with a small space and a vice or saw attached to the kitchen table. Unless you are planning to make large frames, however, this is usually adequate for the carpentry involved, and frames can be placed on the floor for glueing.

You do not require a great deal of expensive equipment at the outset; you can begin with a small range of hand tools and acquire more sophisticated items as the need arises. The expansion in the do-it-yourself industry has forced manufacturers to become more and more competitive, which has resulted in a wide range of tools becoming accessible to the amateur enthusiast.

The tools that the professional framemakers use, namely foot-operated guillotine cutters (Morso cutters), and the underpinning machines for joining the frame together have been designed for speed and yield perfect frames within minutes. However, they are both large and expensive, and are not relevant for most home-based framemakers.

SAWS AND CUTTERS

The Morso cutter is probably the machine most widely used by professional framemakers. It is a very well designed machine and has been in existence for over forty years with very little modification. It does take up a large amount of space, but there are now some smaller versions of the same basic design which are hand operated and can be clamped onto a small table.

The most essential tool for the home-based framemaker is a good mitre saw which is mounted onto a metal base and held in place by two steel columns. There are now many makes available and they are very reasonably priced. These have largely replaced the traditional wood or metal mitre boxes used with a tenon saw. The wooden boxes tend to erode at the edges with use and consequently give inaccurate cuts. The metal ones are better, and when used with a good-quality saw yield accurate results, but they are more difficult to use than mitre saws and so have declined in popularity.

Morso cutter
This has two blades mounted onto a moving block, which is operated by foot, and cuts two mitres at the same time.

Trimmer
The trimmer is useful if you are cutting moulding with a saw. It is used to slice off small pieces of wood so that the opposite sides of the frame are equal.

Underpinner
1 When pre-decorated mouldings are used, the conventional method of joining frames by nailing is tiresome, as the nail holes have to be filled with a matching-coloured filler. Underpinning machines dispense with the need for nailing. They fire staples into the frame from the back without leaving any mark on the sides.

2 Glueing and underpinning are done as part of the same process, with the frame in place on a flat desk. The underpinner shown here is a large professional type, but small hand-operated models are now being developed for the do-it-yourself market.

Mitre saw

The mitre saw is the most important tool for the home-based framemaker. Accurate mitre cuts can be made easily, and most mitre saws have a built-in protractor so that the angle can be changed for cutting octagons and so on. Most also have a metal arm attached, enabling you to cut a second piece of moulding exactly the same size as the first without measuring.

HAND TOOLS

After you have cut the frame it must be glued, and the mitre joints held firmly with some form of a cramp or clamp.

To help you complete the frame it is useful to have a few hand tools. A drill, whether hand or electric, is essential, particularly for hardwoods. It is almost impossible to nail into a hardwood frame without first drilling a hole. For softwood frames, a bradawl is usually adequate to make a pilot hole for the nail to sit in before it is driven in by the hammer. These come in a variety of sizes and types but are basically spikes with wooden handles.

There are many types of pliers, and it is useful though not essential to have a selection. The pincer type is good for extracting bent and broken nails, and the snub-nosed engineering or electrical pliers for nail straightening and cutting.

A tack hammer, sometimes called a pin hammer, is essential for nailing the sides of the frame, as is a punch for driving the nail below the surface of the wood. This hole is then filled, sanded and decorated to match the finish of the frame. Punches come in many shapes and sizes, but one general-purpose punch is all that you need. Those with recessed heads are the most useful type.

The glue most commonly used by framemakers is the quick setting PVA (polyvinyl acetate) type. Because of its strength and quick-bonding quality this has largely replaced the traditional animal glues that need to be mixed and heated. There are many other types of strong glue such as epoxy resins and casein glues which are also suitable for joints. All glue perishes in time, as one can see on old frames, where there are gaps or movement in the joints. For this reason it is very important to use nails or other supports as well.

Strap-type frame clamp

Corner pieces for clamp

Vice

Cordless electric drill

Hand drill

Punch

Pliers

Bradawl

Tack (pin) hammer

G-clamp

Steel rule

T-square

Strap clamp
These all-in-one clamps are made in both steel and plastic. This plastic one is adequate for most frames, though for heavier mouldings you may need a steel one, which exerts more pressure.

Spring mitre clips
These are particularly useful for joining awkward profiles such as those with a shallow outside edge, which tend to pop out of the tape of the all-in-one clamps because there is not enough surface area.

Corner clamps
The traditional corner clamps are suitable for most moulding, but like the strap-type clamps, they do have difficulty with reverse style mouldings and any others with shallow outside edges.

MOUNT CUTTERS

An entire industry has developed around the cutting of bevelled edges for the window apertures of mounts.*

Traditionally this was done by hand, using a sharp knife and a steel straight edge, but it takes practice and considerable skill to cut bevels in this way. The devices now available range from the elaborate bench cutting machines used by professionals to a variety of hand-held cutters.

The American-made Dexter hand-held cutter, which has been in existence for many years, is versatile and well-suited to the beginner. It is heavy enough to cut through the mountboard in one push, and can also be used to cut ovals and circles.

The Logan cutter gives a generous bevel and will also cut through in one pass. At the present time it is probably the most sophisticated hand-held cutter available.

The Olfa mount cutter is inexpensive and easy to use. The perspex base allows you to see the line as you cut, but the lack of weight means that you have to repeat the cut two or three times.

The Maped cutter comes closest to the professional bench cutters. It has a cutter mounted onto a ruler that is used for measuring the window aperture as well as holding the cutter in place.

Each year different designs appear in the shops. They all need a little practice, but in time will yield good results.

*FURTHER INFORMATION

Cutting the mount   page 24

▲ This simple cutter, a Cushway, has the same action as the Dexter cutter and uses the same blades. The blades can be mounted at either end, so this is a useful cutter for left-handed people.

▲ The Olfa cutter has a perspex base, which allows you to see the line as you cut the bevel. The triangular blades are designed to cut through the board in two or three passes.

▼ This is an adaptation of a small Logan cutter, with a rule that allows you to cut without drawing lines first.

▼ The Maped cutter works on the same principle as the larger bench cutters, and also comes with a vertical cutter for straight lines.

▲ The professional bench cutters are quick and easy to use, and cut good wide bevels. Unfortunately, however, they are considerably more expensive than the others shown here.

▲ **Oval and circle cutter**
This professional circle and oval cutter has adjustable measuring arms so that different dimensions and shapes can be cut.

MOULDING SHAPES

► The three mouldings at the top are all different variations of the reverse style, with shallow back edges. The middle three are swept mouldings, while those at the bottom have flat sections. The latter type is useful for veneering, as wood veneers cannot be applied over intricate shapes or sharp curves.

There are many different types of frame profiles with widths varying from a narrow strip to several inches, but they can be divided into a few main categories.

The swept frame has a high outside edge that sweeps down in a curve to the sight edge. These have been used in the past as foundations for elaborate moulded decoration, but they can be used in a plainer manner as a natural wood finished frame, and are perennially popular.

The opposite shape to the swept frame is the reverse profile. This has the highest part of the moulding near to the picture and has the effect of thrusting the picture forward. This type of shape has been known since the 16th century and is still popular and widely used today.

The border frame or *cassetta type combines a flat border within the profile. These borders lend themselves to many styles of decoration, or for more contemporary pictures, can be left plain.

REVERSE MOULDING

FLAT MOULDINGS

SWEPT MOULDINGS

CASSETTA-STYLE MOULDING

THE PARTS OF THE FRAME

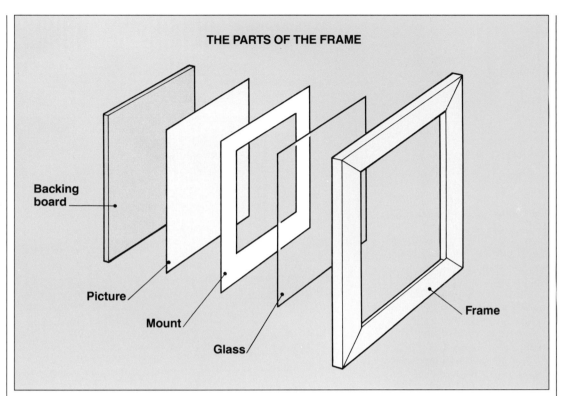

Backing board

Picture

Mount

Glass

Frame

CUSHION MOULDINGS

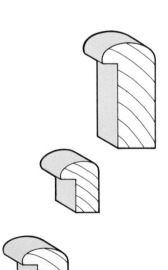

THE PARTS OF THE MOULDING

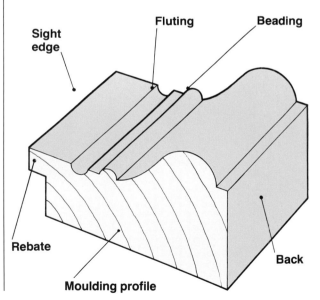

Sight edge

Fluting

Beading

Rebate

Moulding profile

Back

DECORATED MOULDINGS

The industry in pre-decorated mouldings has greatly expanded in recent years, and tends to follow the fashion of interior designs in interior decoration, fabrics and furniture. It is only possible to include a few examples of the vast range available.

Care must be taken when using pre-decorated mouldings, as many have a high gloss or fragile finish which can easily be damaged in the cutting and nailing process.

The range of pre-decorated mouldings is constantly increasing, so it is worth looking around to find out what different suppliers can offer. Mouldings like these, however, some of which have been designed by a leading framemaking business for their own use, are very expensive, and you may find it ultimately more satisfying – as well as less costly – to decorate your own frames.

▲ This range of stained and veneered wood mouldings with gilt sight edges shows the popular colours and shapes of natural-wood frames.

▶ Limed, veneered, stained and ebonized natural wood finishes as well as more richly coloured and gilded finishes are now available as pre-decorated mouldings. Traditional shapes and colours as well as contemporary designs are included in most manufacturers' catalogues.

▲ Soft pastel colours have been lightly washed onto the mouldings so that the natural grain of the wood is still visible. Gold foil sight edges add a touch of contrast.

CHAPTER 2

MAKING
A SIMPLE
FRAME

The basic wood-cutting, joinery and mount-cutting skills needed to make a simple frame are elementary and can be learnt in an afternoon. Obviously practice will improve your technique, and once you have gained competence and confidence you can attempt more complex joinery as and when needed.

The primary consideration at the outset is accuracy of measurement. Well-cut and measured pieces of wood slot together effortlessly. It is always possible to force badly cut joints together and to fill resulting cracks and holes with fillers, but the frames are never satisfactory. Even the unpractised eye picks up a very small discrepancy in the squareness of a frame when it is hung on a wall. Also, if the frame is not square, then the mount, glass and backing board all have to be cut with the same error to fit the frame. You can minimize this type of mistake by double checking before joining the frame together.

Aesthetic considerations, however, are equally important. However well a frame is made it will not be satisfactory unless it performs its other function, which is that of enhancing the image. There are many different ways to frame a picture, and a large variety of mouldings and mount boards available, so it is wise to take time over deciding which style best suits the picture. Professional framemakers will have samples to hand, but this is seldom a possibility for the home framemaker, so until you gain experience you will find it helpful to take the picture with you when you choose mounts and mouldings.

CUTTING THE MOUNT

First check that the mount board is square. If it has come directly from a manufacturer or supplier it is bound to be, but if you are using an off-cut it is essential to check. This is done by measuring the diagonals. If there is a discrepancy and it is not obvious where it is, a new right angle must be established and all subsequent measurements taken from this.

Give some thought to the proportions of mount to picture, as you don't want it to appear either swamped or crowded. It is usual to allow a larger margin at the bottom than at the sides and top. This is to correct an optical illusion which occurs when the picture is hung on the wall: if all the margins are the same width the bottom one looks smaller than the others. A minor adjustment is all that is necessary, but some frame-makers prefer to have a considerably larger margin at the base of the picture for reasons of presentation. This is a matter of personal taste.

Cutting the window

It is a straightforward matter to cut a window with squared edges, but most mounts are cut with bevelled edges, which looks more attractive.

In the past, bevels were cut with a sharp knife and a steel straightedge, but this is not easy, which is why there are now so many mount cutters on the market. Most of these work on a similar principle, with one or two variations. The Dexter and other similar hand-held cutters have blades which are pushed along a straightedge, and are designed so that you can cut on the reverse of the mount to avoid damage to the front surface. The measurements are also marked on the reverse. When cutting on the reverse, start the cut at the bottom left corner and continue clockwise around the mount (if you were cutting on the front you would start at the bottom right corner and work anti-clockwise).

If you prefer to use the traditional knife and straight-edge method, try to find a small sharp knife that feels comfortable in your hand. There is a large selection of craft knives available in tool and graphic supply shops.

Hold the knife as you would a pen, with the back of the blade resting against the bevel of the straightedge. Pierce the window aperture in the corner with the point of the blade. Do not go too deep and try to cut through the card in one pass. It is easier to first make a pilot cut, just lightly scoring the card, and then cut through in one or two passes after that. If you are cutting on the reverse of the mount you will need to overcut the corners by the depth of the mount card. When all the sides have been cut, any rough areas can be smoothed down with fine sandpaper.

Using a mountcutter
1 Before you measure out the mount, put the picture on the board and move it around until you find the right width of margin. Cut the board to the outside measurement and then mark out those for the window aperture.

2 Double-check all the measurements, and make sure the window aperture is square at the corners by measuring the diagonals. The Dexter mountcutter used here cuts 0.7 mm away from the straightedge, so a further mark is made to ensure that the cutter is correctly aligned. If you use a different mountcutter, read the instructions carefully before you begin.

3 When cutting on the back of the card, as here, the window must be overcut at the corners by the thickness of the card. Press the cutter through the card, align the straightedge to the mark, and slowly move the cutter along the line, working clockwise around the mount from the bottom left-hand corner.

SECURING PICTURE TO MOUNT

▶ If you cut another piece of mountboard the same size as the mount you can fix the picture to this by making a hinge from small pieces of gumstrip or acid-free tape.

▶ However, the picture can be fixed directly to the back of the mount as shown here. Use as little adhesive tape as possible; the glass and backing board will hold the mount and picture in place.

Back of mount

Back of picture

Folded adhesive tape

Sheet of card

Back of picture

Back of mount

Adhesive tape

4 Before removing the piece cut out for the window make sure that it is not sticking anywhere, or you may tear it. The Dexter cutter will go through the board at one push, but with other types you may need to make two or three shallow cuts. When the window is complete any rough edges can be smoothed with fine-grade sandpaper.

Using a knife
To cut bevelled windows in the traditional manner with a knife and straightedge requires some practice, as well as a sharp-bladed knife that is comfortable to hold. When cutting on the reverse of the mount, work from the inside, placing the straightedge on the line marked for the top of the aperture, with the bulk of the card towards you. Make a series of cuts, remembering to overcut the corners by the thickness of the card.

CUTTING THE FRAME

Both ends of each piece of moulding must be cut at a 45° angle so that each corner slots together to form 90° (called a mitre joint). The other requirement is that the opposite sides are precisely equal in size; if there are discrepancies the corners will not fit tightly and the frame will be weak.

Accurate measuring is thus very important. To calculate the frame size, first measure the picture size, or if a mount-board surround is being used the external mount size. Next measure the width of the back of the moulding, not including the rebate*. These two measurements, the image or mount size and the width of the moulding, provide the formula for measuring the frame size, which is simply the image or mount size plus twice the width of the back edge of the moulding plus a small allowance for a comfortable fit (about 3 mm/$\frac{1}{8}$ in). These measurements refer to the outer edge of the moulding.

Cutting the frame
This procedure is the same whether you are using a simple wood or metal mitre box or the more sophisticated mitre saws. Not all mouldings can be held in the same

manner. For example, a swept shape with a high outside edge is most easily held with the edge at the back of the box or mitre saw, while a reverse-style moulding with a low outside edge is easier to secure if the edge is towards you as you cut and the rebated edge securely held against the back.

Whichever way you decide to hold the moulding, the bottom must always be in contact with the surface of the box or saw. If it is tilted, the angle of the cut will not be correct. When you have a long length of moulding or a wide or awkward piece to cut, you may need to clamp the wood with G-clamps.

First cut the mitre at one end of the moulding, and then measure from that cut. Mark off on the long edge of the frame, and then use a try square to mark a perpendicular line down the outside edge. Make the next cut on this line.

When you have cut the first side you can use it as a template for your next measurement, repeating the same procedure for the opposite pair of sides. Finally, compare the opposite sides face to face to make sure that the cuts are accurate. If you have access to a trimmer*, any small errors can be corrected easily, otherwise adjustments can sometimes be made with a mitre saw. In some cases, however, where the error is too small to trim with a saw you may have to cut another piece of moulding.

✱FURTHER INFORMATION

| The parts of the moulding | page 19 |
| Saws and cutters | page 12 |

1 The frame can be made before the mount is cut, but it is easier and more reliable to take the measurements from the mount. Make a note of them as you measure, as it is easy to make mistakes.

2 Cut the first mitre and then mark the position for the other one with a pencil mark on the outer edge of the frame, double-checking before cutting. Never try to measure out a whole length for cutting; mark and cut one strip at a time.

3 The mitre saw should be fixed to a workbench or sturdy table so that there is not too much movement as you cut. Place the moulding in the saw, making sure that the bottom edge of the frame is resting on the cutting surface. Use the saw gently; a slow motion will yield more accurate cuts than a fast and furious attack.

6 Before joining (see following pages) the ash moulding is stained to harmonize with colours in the picture. This can be done after joining, but it is easier to apply the stain when the wood is in separate pieces. After joining you may need to smooth the corners with sandpaper, and this will damage the stain.

4 When all the lengths have been cut, place each pair face to face to check the accuracy of the cuts. If there is a serious discrepancy you can recut the mitre, but it is seldom possible to remove an amount smaller than about 3 mm ($\frac{1}{8}$ inch).

5 Do not sandpaper the cut ends, as this will round them and prevent them joining properly. Rough edges can be removed with a knife or chisel.

FORMULA FOR MEASURING FRAME

Rebate

Back of moulding

This diagram of the back of a finished frame shows how by adding the measurements of the two back edges to the picture size you can measure the outside dimensions of the frame. Remember not to include the rebate in the measurements.

JOINING THE FRAME

Professional framemakers use a machine called an underpinner, which glues and pins the frame in one operation in a matter of minutes. These were developed in response to the rapid growth of the industry in pre-decorated mouldings. Some of these have high-gloss surfaces and elaborate colour finishes which makes it difficult to disguise nail-holes in the sides or the slightly rougher edges of hand-cut mitres.

Underpinners are now becoming less expensive, but most home framers will have to join the frame by hand, first glueing and then nailing the corners. To hold the frame firmly while the glue is drying, you will need some form of clamping jig, and there are now several types available, which join and tighten all four corners of the frame at the same time. In the past, framemakers used to make the frame in two halves, joining each opposite pair of pieces in a vice and nailing them at the same time as glueing. With the modern clamps, the frame is left until the glue is dry and then nailed. It is possible to improvise a clamping jig from rope, or better still, rubber inner tubing or strong elastic, which can be tied around the frame and wedged with wooden blocks for greater tension.

Some moulding shapes, such as reverse mouldings, which have very shallow back edges, are inclined to jump out of a clamping jig, because there is insufficient surface to hold the frame in place. Mitre corner clips can be useful here, but they must be used with caution on pre-decorated mouldings because they leave marks in the corners where the sharp teeth have bitten into the wood.

Nailing and filling

For small frames, thin veneer pins are adequate, but as the size of the frame increases, so should that of the nail. As a rough rule-of-thumb, 2.5 cm (1 in) panel pins should be used for 2.5 cm (1 in) mouldings, 5 cm (2 in) panel pins or lost-head nails for 5 cm (2 in) mouldings and so on.

The nails should be first hammered and then punched in and the holes filled with either a proprietary wood filler or one made from glue and the fine sawdust from your mitre saw. The advantage of this home-made filler is that it will provide a perfect colour match, so if you are using natural wood that you intend to wax or stain it is ideal.

Finally, the corners should be rubbed down to neaten the outer edges of the joints, after which the frame is ready to be decorated in any way you choose, or left as natural wood with a coat of varnish or polish.

1 Before clamping, PVA wood glue is applied to the cut ends. This is strong and quick drying, and is now the adhesive most commonly used for all woodwork, though animal glues, epoxy resins and casein glues can also be used. Make sure that the rebate is covered with glue as well as the main part of the frame. When the frame is in the clamp, excess glue can be removed with a damp rag.

2 These all-in-one clamps exert pressure evenly around the frame and are easy to operate. This is a plastic clamp with plastic tape, which is strong enough for most frames. Put the four sides of the frame together on a flat surface and position the corners before tensioning the strap to take up the slack and pushing the small levers out. These act as a brake so that the final tightening can be done with the handle on the main body.

3 A soft wood such as pine can be nailed through without drilling; you will only need a bradawl to make a pilot hole. Hardwoods, however, need to be drilled first, as otherwise the frame could fall apart with the impact of the hammer. With the frame supported in a vice, use a drill the same size as your nails, and penetrate the wood a little less than the depth of the nail.

5 When the nails have been driven two-thirds of the way in, use a punch to knock them in fully. This protects the frame from hammer blows. Punch the nails a little below the surface so that the holes can be covered. Some punches have recessed heads that fit over the head of the nail; these are the easiest to use.

4 On small frames one nail in each corner is adequate, but larger frames will need two or more. These are often nailed from either side so that the nails cross.

6 After the nails have been punched in, the small holes should be filled with wood filler, which can be bought in a range of colours to match the wood used. When the filler is dry the corners are smoothed with sandpaper, but take care not to use too much pressure or the edges will become rounded.

CUTTING THE GLASS

Although most home framemakers will prefer to go to their local glaziers and have pieces of glass cut to size, it is useful to know how to cut and trim glass. If you make a mistake and find that the glass does not quite fit the frame you can cut it down and use it for another frame. Glass is too expensive to waste.

There are three main types of glass cutter, diamond-headed (used for heavy duty glass), tungsten and steel wheel-headed cutters, the latter being the most commonly available. They normally have six or more wheels mounted on a wooden shaft. When a wheel becomes blunt it can be rotated so that a new one takes its place. Even so, they do not last very long. The tungsten wheels, which are not much more expensive, last far longer.

For most frames 2 mm glass, which is light and reasonably strong, is used. For very large areas of glass in a frame you may have to purchase either heavy duty (4 or 5 mm) glass or perspex. Beyond a certain size, approximately 1 metre (39 in) square, light glass is difficult to hold and can wobble in the middle and break. Thicker glass is more rigid.

1 Glass can be measured in the normal way with a ruler and T-square, but in this case the frame has already been joined, so the glass is held against the back of the frame and marked with a felt-tipped pen.

2 Make sure the cutting surface is smooth, as any lumps or bumps underneath will shatter the glass as you cut. Place a steel straightedge, preferably with a non-slip bottom, on the line. Lubricate the wheel in oil, white spirit or methylated spirits and score the glass. Practise on some scrap glass first so that you find out how much pressure to apply.

CUTTING AN OVAL

1 There are professional oval and circle cutters, but these are too expensive for occasional use. Here an oval cardboard template is used to guide the cutter around the curve.

2 Once the glass has been scored all the way round, tap vigorously with the other end of your glass cutter to loosen the oval shape from the surrounding glass.

3 If scoring and tapping does not release the oval, make a series of cuts from the edge of the oval to the outside edge of the glass. These sections can then be broken piece by piece around the oval.

3 Most pictures under glass are framed with the standard 2 mm glass, which does not require a lot of pressure. After scoring the glass, tap vigorously along the line of the cut. This makes it easier to break the glass cleanly. Many cutters have a round knob at the end of the stem.

4 It is important to score the glass only once. If you recut over your last scored mark the glass may break unevenly, and you will blunt the wheel. Here the glass is held with the thumbs on either side of the scored line and pressure is exerted from both sides. This should break the glass easily.

5 Another method of breaking glass, which is rather safer than holding it in your hands, is to place it on a flat ruler or straightedge and press either side. The scored mark must be very closely aligned to the edge of the ruler before downwards pressure is exerted.

6 Sometimes the glass needs to be trimmed. Small pieces cannot be broken in the same way because there is insufficient surface area, so special glass-breaking pliers are used, placed on the score line. If the glass does not break in one long piece, persevere along the cut, breaking off small sections at a time.

FINAL ASSEMBLY

Once all the component parts of the frame are ready, the only task that remains is to cut a backing board from hardboard, plywood or thick cardboard. Hardboard is probably the best choice, as plywood must be cut with a saw, and tends to splinter at the edges. To cut hardboard, mark the cutting line, score it on both sides with a sharp knife and then break it.

It may be necessary to bevel the edges of the hardboard at the back so that it fits into the frame; some pre-decorated mouldings are too shallow to accommodate the "sandwich" of glass, picture and backing board. This can be done with either a plane or a rasp.

Before assembling the frame, make sure that the glass is thoroughly clean on both sides and that there are no marks on the front of the mount. If there are, clean them off with a soft eraser. Attach the picture to the back of the mount with acid-free tape or gumstrip, either of which can be removed if necessary.

Place the frame upside down on a clean, flat surface, put the glass into it and attach some gumstrip to the outer edges of the glass so that it is hidden by the rebate. This acts as a barrier to prevent dust entering from the front of the frame.

Put the mount and picture into the frame, and finally the backing board, then pick up the whole assembly carefully and turn it round to check that the image and mount are centrally placed and there is no dust trapped behind the glass.

To secure the backing board, small nails need to be hammered into the inner edges of the frame to hold the package together. If the wood is very hard you will find it easier to make small pilot holes with a bradawl. Professional framemakers have glazing guns that shoot flat points into the edges of the frame. These machines do save a lot of time, particularly if you have a lot of frames to assemble.

Finally, to prevent dust entering from the back of the frame, apply more gumstrip to cover the join between the backing board and the frame.

1 This photograph shows the component parts of the finished frame: the wooden moulding of stained ash; 2 mm picture glass; an ivory window mount with the print attached, and finally a backing board of hardboard.

2 The glass is fitted into the frame and secured with gumstrip to prevent dust entering from the front. Be careful with the placing of the gumstrip: it should cover the side of the frame and only the thin margin of glass covered by the rebate.

3 The mount with the picture attached is put in place, followed by the backing board, which is secured by nailing small panel pins around the frame. These can be driven in with a punch, but this is not essential. Take care not to aim the hammer downwards, or you could break the glass.

4 To seal the whole unit thoroughly and prevent any dust entering, the small gap between the backing board and the frame should be sealed with gumstrip. Never use masking tape, as it will begin to peel off after quite a short time.

5 The back should look as neat and presentable as the front. Trim the gumstrip neatly, and if the backing board level is lower than the back of the frame, make a small cut in the gumstrip so that it lies as close as possible to the frame.

6 Screw eyes for hanging should be placed approximately a quarter of the way down the frame, and screwed firmly into the moulding. Finally brass wire is tied to both screw eyes and tensioned. Nylon cord can also be used.

FIXINGS AND HANGINGS

1 Brass screw eyes
2 Nylon cord
3 Double picture hooks and pins
4 Mirror plates
5 Chain
6 Chrome screw eyes
7 Single picture hooks and pins
8 Picture rail hooks
9 Picture wire

There are many ways to hang frames and a variety of different fixings can be obtained. The most simple are screw eyes in various sizes, which are screwed into the back of the frame. These should be placed approximately a quarter of the height of the picture away from the top of the frame. If they are placed any further down the picture will hang at an angle from the wall. Brass wire or strong nylon cord can be attached between these two eyes, and the frame is then hung from picture pins, hidden behind the frame. An alternative is to attach lengths of cord or chain and hang the frame from a picture rail.

For heavy frames, hanging plates, sometimes called mirror plates, are often used. These are screwed to the frame and the wall, and generally have two holes for screws into the frame and one hole for a screw into the wall. There are also hanging plates that are flush fitting so that no screws are visible from the front. They are keyhole shaped and are screwed to the back of the frame. At the top of the keyhole a small hole is drilled so that it can hang on a wall screw.

CHAPTER 3

ADVANCED JOINERY

M ost frames are made with mitred corners, because decorative mouldings look more attractive when the moulding profile is continuously maintained around the corners of the frame. From a structural point of view, however, the mitre joint has an obvious limitation. There is no connecting wood across it, and it is necessary to rely on glue and nails for strength.

There are ways in which the mitres can be re-inforced, but there are also frames that do not need mitres, and where stronger structural joints can be used. This chapter discusses more unusual and complex frames and their underlying structures.

HOME-MADE PROFILES

In spite of the large numbers of different moulding designs now available it can sometimes be impossible to find the perfect shape for a particular frame. This problem can be solved either by making your own mouldings using a router or combination plane, or by buying flat sections of wood and decorative beading and sticking them together.

Combination planes, or multi-planes, are essentially groove- and rebate-cutting planes with extra cutters for decorations such as flutes and reeds. Although they have largely been replaced with the faster and more versatile routing power tools, they are still manufactured.

Routers are becoming increasingly used by home-based carpenters, both to cut moulding and for grooving and rebating work. They are fast and quite easy to use and their popularity has kept their prices competitive.

For those framemakers without the facilities or means to use elaborate hand and power tools, there is still the option to make original profiles by combining existing wood shapes bought from local builder's suppliers. Many attractive frames can be made in this manner.

Using a router
1 To cut out a rebate, set the cutting head to the required depth and push the router smoothly along the wood section. It is also possible to cut a rebate after the frame has been assembled.

2 Routers can be fitted with a large range of edge-forming cutters. Here a beading cutter is pushed along the edge of the moulding to create a round edge with a shallow groove either side. Other common edge cutters include chamfer, ogee and cove shapes. There is also a range of cutters for decorating the top surface of the frame, from simple grooves to more elaborate shapes.

Composite profiles
1 A flat piece of ash is chosen as the central border of the frame. In this case, a 7.5 cm (3 inch) section of ash-veneered plywood was cut from a large sheet.

2 To create a rebate, a reeded section of wood was glued onto one edge of the border. It was fastened with masking tape to keep it in place while the glue hardened, and nailed to the central border with thin veneer pins to ensure a strong join.

3 A section of reeded wood, wider than the rebate, but following a similar pattern, was then glued and nailed to the outside of the central margin. Many simple shapes of beading can be obtained from builder's suppliers and used in combination in this way.

Veneer bandings
1 Wood veneers can be used to decorate frames, either as an overall covering or as a border. The underlying moulding must be plain and almost flat, as veneers cannot be bent over a complex shape. Here a "windsor" profile, which has a flat central border, has been chosen.

2 A veneer banding was laid onto the flat border next to the outside edge, and another one, of a different design was laid next to it. These bandings, which are made in a variety of designs and colours, are chiefly used for the decoration of small pieces of furniture and musical instruments.

3 The third piece of banding, the same design as the first, was aligned so that the patterns are parallel. The traditional method of attaching bandings is to chisel out a flat groove so that the banding lies flush with the rest of the wood, but in this case the three bandings fit exactly into the flat margin of the moulding, so it was not necessary.

4 To complete the decoration a strip of machine-carved beads was glued to the sight edge. It is easier to stick the decorative bandings and sections of wood before cutting the frame. Glue them to the wood moulding and strap them tightly with masking tape to ensure that they lie flat and straight.

Wood beads
This strip of machine-cut beads was first gilded with imitation leaf, and is now glued to the sight edge of a stained-oak moulding. The gilt finish on the beads is protected from the masking tape by using strips of paper as a barrier.

VARIOUS JOINTS

There are a number of stronger joints than mitres. These are most often used for frames with flat, undecorated wood sections, and are particularly useful for flat borders within a cassetta-style* frame or for box* frames.

A lap joint is one in which the plain end of one side is set into a rebated cut in the other, and can look attractive in a natural wood finish. Although stronger than a mitre or simple butt joint, it does still need to be pinned.

Corner halving joints are similar in principle, and also need to be glued and reinforced using screws or dowels. The lapped mitre is a more elegant version of the same joint, but has only half the overlap, and is consequently weaker. Both these halving joints are useful for frames with integrated borders, and are considerably stronger than the simple mitre joint. The photographs show various other options.

*FURTHER INFORMATION

Moulding shapes   page 19
Slips and box
   frames   page 46

Mortise and tenon joint
1 This is a very strong joint, and is used for furniture as well as framemaking. It requires accurate cutting for a tight fit and neat appearance.

2 Here the mortise has been pushed through the tenon but not yet glued. The waste wood is marked for cutting.

3 This photograph shows the construction of the joint, with the mortise and tenon both cut. The waste wood, marked with pencil, will be cut away before joining and glueing.

4 The joint has been used for a "window" style frame in beech with a plain bevelled section at the base and an ogee decoration on the other three inner edges.

Lapped mitres
1 These crossed joins are difficult to make, but look very attractive on natural-wood frames. The mitre is strengthened by the lapped halves of the wood, which can be glued and nailed in the normal way. Precise cutting out of the waste wood is essential for a tight join.

Corner halving joint
These joints are similar in principle to the simple lap joint. They can be cut using a hand saw, and need to be glued and pegged or nailed. They are stronger than conventional mitres and are often used on the central margins of cassetta-style frames.

2 Mark a line on the rebated side a half or a third of the width of the wood. Using the other side as a template, mark another line on the inner face and the top and bottom edges. Indicate the waste with a pencil and cut the two lines as neatly as possible. Glue and clamp together and nail through the rebated side.

REINFORCING MITRE JOINTS

A more modern method of reinforcing mitre joints is biscuit joining. The biscuit joiner is a miniature saw that cuts small grooves across joints. A "biscuit" of compressed beech spread with PVA glue is inserted into the groove, and the glue causes the biscuit to expand inside the joint, thus making a very strong bond.

On many old frames you will find that, although the glue has perished, the mitres are still strong due to a traditional method of reinforcement. The mitred corners are glued and pinned in the normal manner, and then a channel is cut across the mitres and a wedge inserted.

Crossover frames

1 Mark out the dimensions of the picture size on the back of the wood and add the required length of the crossover. Indicate the waste wood sections on all crossover sides, and then saw both edges of the cut-out piece. The waste can then be knocked out cleanly with a sharp chisel. The rebate can be cut with a power router or a plough plane. If a plane is used, it is easiest to make the rebate before the frame is assembled, but a router with a right-angle fence can cut it after joining, and rounded corners can be cut square with a chisel.

Rustic crossovers

1 This more traditional crossover frame, also for a sampler, is made of oak. It is made in the same way as the limed ash frame, with the waste wood being cut and chiselled out of the moulding.

2 After glueing, the crossovers can be pegged with wooden dowels or nailed from the back for greater strength. There are no fixed rules for the proportions of the crossover sections, but in general they do not usually exceed a quarter of the frame's length.

3 A small flower ornament has been moulded in composition (see page 136) as a decorative boss for the corners of the frame.

2 The sides of the frame are decorated with stopped chamfer cuts, which are repeated on the crossover sections. These can be made with a sharp chisel or with a router. This type of decoration is well suited to an unsophisticated subject such as a cross-stitch embroidery.

3 The frame has been used to display a child's sampler. The thick oak section has stopped chamfer decorations on the sides and at the crossed corners. It has been stained a darker colour to give the appearance of mature oak. A gilded slip has been added to keep the sampler away from the glass.

ORNAMENTAL EXTENDED CORNERS

This ornamental device, in which the decorative moulding is extended at the corners to form squares outside the main frame, has been used in many ways since the Renaissance. Although the style is usually associated with period frames, it can be equally striking used with modern mouldings.

With careful measuring all the cuts can be carried out using a simple mitre saw, but the cuts must be absolutely precise. If the opposite sections of the extended corners are not identical the frame will look lopsided and unsightly.

In spite of the difficulties it is well worth persevering with ornamental corners, as you can vary the basic idea to make many different styles. For example, some overmantel frames are constructed with extended corners at the top and ordinary mitre joints on the bottom, which gives a pleasing top-heavy appearance to the frame.

1 The sides of the frame are cut in the normal way and then each end is re-cut across the mitre in the opposite direction, starting at the top of the sight edge.

2 To form the extended corners, two triangles of wood are cut for each corner. Each triangle should be the smallest possible section of complete moulding, with two 45° cuts from the sight edge. When glued together they form 90° at the extended corner. Bind them with masking tape or use a mitre corner clip to hold them in place while the glue sets.

3 The small sections of wood that act as a bridge between the main frame and the extended corner are cut next. There are two pieces of wood for each corner, and they are cut in two stages. First measure the width across the sight edge of the extended corner as in step 2; in this example it is approximately 1 cm (³⁄₈ inch). Then make two precise parallel cuts for each section of wood, in opposite directions for each section.

4 The second cut is made across the mitre on the rebate of the small sections of wood. This has to be done delicately because the rebate is liable to break off the frame with the pressure of the saw. This second cut should allow the bridge sections to align neatly with the extended corners. Glue and bind them with masking tape to the extended corners.

5 To join the frame, first glue the main frame together. This is tricky because there is only a narrow joining edge. Once the glue has set, place the extended corners in the same clamp, give them to the main frame and tighten the clamp.

The protruding corners are vulnerable to knocks, so to strengthen them glue and nail small plates of wood or hardboard to the back of the frame.

▲ This frame is one of a pair made by Michele Riley for two 17th century prints. The frames have been painted with a thick black casein paint, and the top line of the sight-edge groove decoration has been picked out in an ivory colour, emphasizing the extended corner decorations.

OVALS AND CIRCLES

Oval and circular frames, both of which are often used for mirrors, are nowadays mostly cut with specialist machinery. The mouldings are cut on a curve and then joined – usually in four pieces – into the finished shape. However, they can also be hand made, using traditional methods.

Small frames can be turned on a lathe, but the larger ones have always exercised the ingenuity of traditional framemakers. The method shown here, which involves glueing a series of pegs onto a board in the required shape* and winding strips of veneer around them, certainly dates back to the 18th century and probably earlier.

*FURTHER INFORMATION

Marking out an
oval   page 57

1 For this method, a wood-and-peg template is made first, with the shape marked by a series of pegs drilled and glued at intervals of approximately 1.3 cm ($\frac{1}{2}$ inch). Thin strips of veneer are measured to the desired depth of the frame and cut with a craft knife.
A few further strips are cut approximately 6 mm ($\frac{1}{4}$ inch) narrower to act as the rebate.

2 The frame is constructed upside down so that the top surface lies flush with the template. A clothes peg is used here to secure one end of the veneer strip to the outside of the pegs.

3 The veneer is then tightly wrapped around the pegs, and glue is applied in between each layer. It is important to keep the veneer flush with the pegs at all times, so that a correct shape is maintained.

6 Here gesso is used as an undercoat for a painted finish. This is thick enough to cover any small blemishes, and also helps to bind the whole frame together.

4 The veneer is wound around the frame until the required thickness is reached. It will need approximately ten rounds to make an inch, with slight variations according to the thickness of the veneer.

7 Finally, the frame has been given a distressed-paint finish, achieved by painting on two separate coats and rubbing down the second one (green) with fine sandpapers and wire wool to reveal the base coat. The red undercoat was protected with an acrylic matt varnish so that it remained intact during the distressing process. (See Distressed paint effects, page 90.)

5 When the frame has reached the required width, it is left to dry and set for a few hours. it can be secured with strips of masking tape. The many layers of veneer will leave a ridged surface on the frame, which can be smoothed with a plane and sandpaper.

SLIPS AND BOX FRAMES

Slip frames, which have an inner piece to isolate the picture from the glass, can either be used in a purely functional way, to prevent the picture sticking to the glass and causing damage, or as an extra decoration.

Slips can also be used as fillers for frames that are too large. They can be bought in many different shapes and finishes.

Box frames

These are mainly used to frame objects, for instance medals, jewellery, butterflies and other small-scale items, but they can also create a dramatic effect for pictures, making them appear as though in a presentation cabinet.

It is necessary to have moulding of sufficient depth to trap the glass at the front, leaving a gap between it and the artwork, which is secured at the base of the frame. The glass can be held in place with slips, either visible or hidden, which are attached to the sides of the frame.

There are some specially deep mouldings manufactured for this purpose, but you can also modify existing mouldings with an extra section of wood on the bottom.

Textile frames

1 This is the flat central border of a cassetta-style frame, which was surfaced with canvas, with gesso on top. It is now painted with an indigo emulsion to contrast with the warm colours of the textile.

2 The inner frame was painted with shellac and bronze pigments before being fitted to the central border. This needs to be cut carefully to fit tightly inside the flat moulding. It is possible to buy or make moulding with a double rebate for this purpose.

3 Finally the outer frame of stained and varnished wood is fitted around the border piece. This both protects the inner frames and adds another colour and shape to the composite frame. For extra security the frames can be glued and nailed together.

4 The textile, which has been attached to a wooden panel, is fitted into the frame without glass. Glass can be used, and frequently is, since it protects the fabric from dust and dirt, but it can detract from the overall appearance, making it more difficult to see the fine stitched texture.

Stretching embroidery
Before framing stitched embroidery, it is sometimes necessary to stretch it. Robust fabric can be stretched in a similar way to artist's canvas, that is, nailed or stapled onto a wooden frame. For more delicate works a backing card can be used as a support, and the fabric can be sewn across the back.

BOX FRAME CONSTRUCTIONS

Rebate

Main frame

Glass

Backing board

◄ This diagram shows a flat section of wood placed inside the rebate as a support for the glass. It is less deep than the frame moulding, thus allowing a space for the picture and backing board.

Thin strip of wood supporting glass

Main frame

Glass

Backing board

◄ This is an alternative arrangement, using a small quadrant wood section behind the glass to hold it in place. This support is not visible from the front. The backing board in this example is attached with screws to the back edge of the frame.

Small quadrant supporting glass

Quadrant slip
In this case a colourful batik on white calico is separated from the glass by using a quadrant slip underneath the glass. The quadrant is the same type of wood as the outer frame and has been stained and polished to match. The photograph shows the reverse of the frame and the stretcher used to display the batik. These stretchers can be made from flat timber, but remember to chamfer the facing edges so that the fabric is not damaged by sharp corners.

Decorative slip
Slips can be used for purely decorative effect, as here, or to separate the glass from the picture. They are also used to pad out existing frames which are too large for a particular picture. They are available in many different shapes, sizes and finishes, and are extremely useful for minor adjustments.

Cabinet style
1 This "shadow box" or cabinet-style frame is used to advantage to display a magnificent ivory fan. The frame is a deep, flat section of wood with small floral ornaments. The dark velvet background contrasts with the ivory and allows all the fine carving to be seen clearly.

2 Dark green velvet-covered slips hold the glass at the front of the box. The back panel of velvet with the ivory fan attached is held at the back of the frame in a rebate formed by the slips and the outer frame. Moveable fasteners hold the back panel in place.

FRAMES WITH AND WITHOUT REBATES

Half-round moulding and flat sections

Flat wood sections

Quadrant and flat sections

▲ To make the frame more interesting, profiled beadings can be used to cover the surface.

◄ Rebates can be created by adding small flat, half round or quadrant sections to plain timber.

FLOATING FRAMES

In this style of frame the picture does not sit behind a rebate in the normal way but stands proud of its protective border. It is particularly effective with panel paintings or artwork where the image extends fully to the edges; because there is no rebate, nothing is hidden.

There are a number of ways to approach the construction of this kind of frame. One is to build a border of wood or composite board around the edge of the painting. As in a mount, the width of this border is chosen to suit the picture. The picture is then secured to this border using a batten that is attached to both. Another section of wood or moulding – an outer "frame" – can be attached to the edges of the border to give both protection and extra emphasis.

Another simple way to construct a floating frame is to cut a piece of flat wood or board to fit precisely around the picture, and then secure the picture from the back using blocks, batons or reinforcing plates. The picture can be presented flush with the border, recessed or projecting forward.

1 This portrait has been painted on a wooden panel, bevelled at the edges. It is now attached to a background of oak-veneered plywood by

2 Both the frame and the background have been sealed with shellac and then waxed, so that the warm, natural colours of the wood complement the warmer tones in the portrait.

FIXING PICTURE TO FRAME

▲ This diagram shows the back of the floating frame shown on page 80. A simple wood section was constructed around a picture painted on a wooden panel. A framework of wooden struts was then attached to the back of the panel and fixed to the frame with metal reinforcing plates.

▲ This example shows a batten that has been glued and nailed onto a wooden margin, with a recess on the inside edge. The canvas stretcher support for the picture is then attached with screws to the batten.

PENTAGONS, HEXAGONS AND OCTAGONS

On most mitre saws* a simple protractor is provided with positions indicated for pentagons, hexagons and octagons. They are no more difficult to cut than 45° mitre joints. Some contemporary cramps have versatile corners which can accommodate the various angles, so that these frames can be glued and tightened in the same manner as conventional types. Alternatively sprung mitre clips* can be used.

For pentagons, because of the uneven number of sides, each section of moulding must be the same length, but hexagons and octagons can have different side lengths provided the opposite sides are equal. In this way many interesting shapes can be made, which are particularly attractive for mirrors and decorative work.

✱FURTHER INFORMATION

Saws and cutters   page 12
Using frame clamps   page 13
Liming   page 74

Pentagon
1 This shape was chosen for the five-pointed starfish for obvious reasons, though it can be an effective format for other shapes as well. Unlike the octagons and hexagons, pentagons have to have equal-sized sides.

2 The frame was cut with a mitre saw, set at 54°. The joinery is slightly tricky because the reverse-shaped moulding will not fit into conventional cramps, so mitre corner clips are used.

3 The frame was gessoed and painted with terracotta burnishing clay, after which a coat of black burnishing clay was applied on top and distressed with wire wool to reveal some of the red undercolour. This softens the black surface and picks out the red in the image.

Octagon

1 Sometimes an image can benefit from a less conventional shape than the standard rectangle. This coloured etching has an eight-sided window-aperture mount decorated with wash and pen lines. It is possible to vary the sizes of the sides of an octagon frame, but here all the sides are equal.

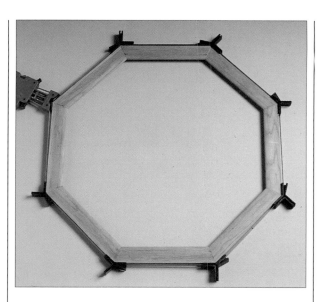

2 A frame of rounded oak moulding has been cut in the same way as the pentagon, but with the saw set at an angle of 67°. For the joinery, an all-in-one clamp is used, with extra corner pieces.

3 The oak frame has been limed to make it more discreet in tone and prevent it dominating the delicate colours of the print. Both frames and etchings are by Derek James.

CHAPTER 4

DECORATIVE MOUNTS

M ounts, which are usually made of cardboard and have bevel-edged window apertures, both present and protect works on paper, such as watercolours, prints and drawings.

The card acts as a barrier between the image and the glass, which is necessary because any moisture present in the atmosphere around the frame can make the glass cling to the paper and cause damage.

Mounts were not widely used until the middle of the 19th century, when cardboard was industrially produced for the first time. Previously, works on paper had sometimes been protected from the glass by small pieces of wood, often the size of matchsticks, which were inserted into the rebate of the frame behind the glass. Another device was to use a slip frame placed behind the glass and in front of the picture. This was usually a bevelled flat section of wood, which was gilded or decorated to suit the picture. Both methods are still used today to present images where mountcard seems inappropriate. Embroideries, for example, often need the protection of glass but are not always suited by a window mount. Similarly, a window mount would not be the best choice for an old document, or any work in which the edges of the paper are an integral part of the overall image. For most pictures on paper, however, a mount is both the easiest and most attractive option.

PROPORTIONS

Whatever colour or decoration you decide on for a mount it will not be successful unless the margins are in pleasing proportion to the image. As mentioned earlier, it is usual to allow a greater depth of margin at the bottom of the picture, but apart from this there are no golden rules about the proportion of mount to picture; your choice will be affected by personal taste, prevailing fashions and the colour of the mountboard. However, it is generally accepted that wide margins look better in neutral colours such as ivory or pale greys, as a large area of strong colour around a picture can swamp it and interfere with our perception of it. It is useful to have a few pieces of board to put around the edges of the picture to see what seems to complement the image.

Small images such as engravings or woodcuts often look more impressive in wide mounts, which add weight and importance to them. In a narrow margin these small images can often be lost and unnoticed. On larger pictures a wide mount may look appropriate, but will sometimes make the overall size of the frame too big for displaying on a wall.

WORKING IT OUT

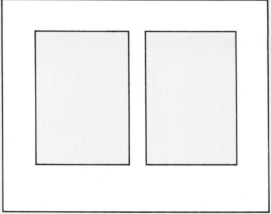

Double windows
When two pictures are framed together, for example two similar prints or paintings of the same subject, the central border needs to be quite narrow, for example approximately half the measurement of the top and side borders. This will separate the images while emphasizing their relationship.

Making a cartoon
It is helpful to work out the proportions by making a "cartoon" like this. You can refer to it while you cut the mount, which will prevent mistakes.

Ovals and circles

Ovals and circles are trickier to mark out and cut than the straight-sided window apertures, but both can be marked with a compass, as shown here.

The Dexter hand-held mountcutter will cut both ovals and circles as long as you make a template, preferably of plywood or hardboard. This should be slightly smaller than the required size (about 0.7 mm) all round, and can be cut with a bandsaw or knife.

Place the template on the face of the mount (it is not possible to cut on the reverse using this process), and secure it with nails or pins. Place the cutter tight against the edge of the template with the blade piercing the board and gently push it around the template. Circles are easier than ovals because the curve is constant, while an oval changes curves as it approaches the apex, and it is easy to slide away from the edge of the template.

There are professional oval and circle cutters that are easy to use, but are too expensive for the home-based framemaker. In recent times a new hand-held oval and circle cutter has been developed by Daler, who manufacture mountboard. This is an ingenious device, similar in principle to professional cutters but smaller in size and a fraction of the price.

Marking an oval
1 Decide the width and height of the oval aperture required. Mark out both measurements, being careful to draw straight lines that intersect at 90°. Take half the measurement of the longest side. Mark off the measurements onto the longest side from the end of the shortest side, using a compass.

2 Hammer thin nails into the intersecting points of the measurements on the longest side. Take a piece of string or some strong thread and make a loop around both nails. The loop should be tied at the outside of the long measurement and reach the furthest nail.

Cutting with a template
1 Here the method has been used to cut a template in stiff cardboard which has been nailed onto the mount board in the correct position. The Dexter cutter cuts 0.7mm away from the straightedge, and so the template has to be cut that much smaller all round. It is not possible to cut on the back of the mount for this procedure.

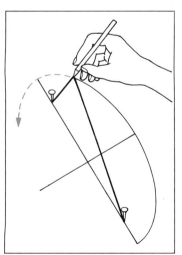

3 Place a pencil inside the loop and pull it tight. Then slowly push the pencil around the loop.

2 Place the cutter carefully against the template and pierce the board with the blade. Push the cutter slowly all round the template, paying special attention to the change of curvature at the apex of the oval. When you have cut all round the oval it should come out of the mount board easily. Any rough edges can be smoothed with fine-grade sandpaper.

DOUBLE AND TREBLE MOUNTS

Double and treble mounts can enhance the presentation of the picture by adding greater depth and colour possibilities. There are many variations of complementary and contrasting colours. Sometimes a colour in the picture can be echoed in the thin margin of colour that forms the inner border of a double mount, while on other occasions a contrasting colour can be used for dramatic effect.

The conventional arrangement of proportions is that the inner mount or mounts have the same margins on all sides, while the outer mount has a greater margin at the bottom. If you are using a bright colour for an inner margin it may be enough to have a centimetre or less showing; any more might conflict with the picture.

Where there are many colours in the picture, or where there is no obvious predominant colour, it may be safer to use neutral colours for the inner margins. Double mounts can be very effective when both inner and outer mounts are the same colour, particularly when a neutral ivory or grey is used against a colourful pastel or watercolour. The bevels form slight shadows around the inner mount, giving a discreet hint of soft and subtle decoration.

Treble mounts expand the possibilities of colour variations, for example you could use two shades of blue, grey or ivory with a slip of bright red in the middle. Sometimes the inner mount is gilded or decorated with marbled paper while the outer mount is left plain.

Double and treble mounts do, of course, entail more work in the drawing out and cutting, and you will need to measure very carefully. A small error of judgement on a single mount may escape attention, but on a double or treble one any mistakes are amplified by the other windows. The inner mounts need only be a little wider than the visible margins, and can be taped to the back of the outer mount.

▲ A double mount enhances the presentation of a picture by adding depth. It also enables you to experiment with different colour combinations. Here two shades of blue are used, the darker one on the inside.

▲ In this example two colours of mountboard have been doubled in thickness to increase the size of the bevels. It is not difficult to glue two pieces of card together, and the joins are barely noticeable when the bevel has been cut.

▲ This double mount has a decorative inner mount, wider than normal to accommodate the decoration. The "wash line" is actually an extra border of sprayed paint edged with gold lines. A margin the same width as the decoration was cut out of a piece of scrap card to act as a mask while the spraying was done.

▲ In this treble mount a thin slip of red is sandwiched between a grey and an ivory board. A bright colour can be used in small quantities without interfering with the image. Great care must be taken in the measurements of double and treble mounts because the slightest error shows up.

UNUSUAL SHAPES

Shaped window apertures can suit some pictures, particularly if the window echoes a contour in the image. They are more difficult to execute with hand-held cutters than standard mounts, and templates have to be used for curves.

1 This simple device adds a little square decoration to the corners of the window aperture.

2 This decorative cut-out has another coloured card used both as a double mount and as a background for the cuts.

3 The spraying method was used here to decorate the inner mount. The bevel was sprayed as well, and masks of right-angled triangles were placed at the corners to "reserve" white areas, which were then edged with a fine black line.

4 A complex shape of curves and straight lines are joined together, and amplified with a decorative gold line.

VARIETIES OF MOUNTBOARD

Most mountboard is made from wood pulp and faced with coloured paper. A wide variety of coloured and decorated boards is now available, ranging from flat colours to marbled, textured and fabric effects. The more decorative boards tend to follow fashions in the world of interior design, and change from time to time.

All the industrially made mounts, whatever the finish, will reveal a plain card bevel when cut. This can be a pleasant contrast to the surface decoration, but you may prefer an overall colour or texture that includes the bevel, in which case you must decorate the mount* yourself.

Board weight
The thickness of mountboard is expressed in "sheet" size, and the most generally available board is usually between 4 and 10 sheet. It is not always easy to find thicker board unless you go to a specialist supplier, but one way to make a heavier mount is to glue two sheets together before cutting. When the bevelled window is cut the joins are not obvious, and the extra depth of the bevel can be attractive. It is, of course, a little harder to cut through two mounts.

Conservation board
Unfortunately, much mountboard is still made of unrefined groundwood pulp, which contains acids and can be harmful to works on paper. The "burning" by the acid takes place over a long period of time, so for temporary items such as posters or cheap prints it is not necessary to purchase the more expensive acid-free or acid-neutral board. For a picture, map or document of any value, however, acid-free conservation board should always be used. The popularity of this has lowered the price and increased the colour range in recent years, and conservation gum tapes and glues have also been brought out to help preserve particularly valuable pictures.

✱FURTHER INFORMATION

Fabric mounts   page 66
Special finishes   page 68
Broken-colour effects page 69

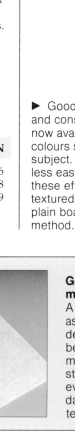

▶ Good-quality mountboard and conservation board are now available in a range of colours suitable for almost any subject. Textured boards are less easy to obtain, but for these effects you can glue textured paper or fabric onto plain board, or use the gesso method.

Gesso texture on mounts
A thick mixture of gesso, as used for pastiglia decoration (see p.120) can be used to texture the mountboard. This can be stippled on, giving an even, grainy surface, dabbed on for greater texture, or combed or scratched in patterns. It is best to use thick, high-quality mountboard for this purpose, as thin card may buckle and warp when the gesso dries.

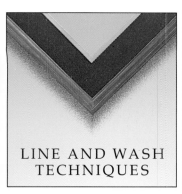

LINE AND WASH TECHNIQUES

Line and wash is a traditional form of decoration associated with watercolours of the late 19th century, and still used for watercolours and other works on paper.

The paint used for the wash line is watercolour, or sometimes thin gouache if an opaque or white line is required. The lines too are often watercolour, drawn on with a pen, though ink is also used. There are no golden rules for the divisions of space between the lines, but commonly the wash line is between 1 cm (⅜ in) and 2 cm (¾ in) and two or three pen lines are grouped very closely together on either side. Picture framers who do a lot of this work usually make or buy an acetate or perspex corner with many pinholes to mark out the various dimensions. This can save a lot of time.

The wash
It is best to paint the wash line first and then edge the borders with a pen line, which gives a crisp quality to the edges. Watercolour is a difficult medium to work with, so if you are a beginner, make a few practice attempts on some scrap board until you get the feel of the paint. It helps to brush the area of the wash with clear water to dampen it, which encourages the colour to settle evenly. Ox gall, a wetting agent used in the manufacture of watercolour, is a useful addition to the watercolour mix (a few drops added to the water is all you need).

Contrary to expectation, it is both easier and faster to brush the colour on freehand rather than using a ruler, but if you feel unable to try without a ruler, turn it upside down so that the bevel edge is on the bottom. This should prevent the ruler picking up colour and dragging it across the board.

It is necessary to brush over the line more than once to achieve a perfectly even wash, so begin with a dilute colour, and a brush of approximately the same width as the wash line. Pull the brush along the border, and keep on going around the wash line until the colour is even and sufficiently dark. Finally, go over the line with clear water and a clean brush, until all corners overlap and other irregularities are blended into the wash.

The pen line
When the wash line is dry, a pen is used with the same or slightly darker colour to sharpen the edges. There are many fine-nibbed, fibre-tipped graphic pens now available in a large range of colours which can be used for this, but the traditional implement is a lining pen. Gold and silver lines can be made by using either water-soluble metallic ink and a lining pen, or one of the gold or silver fibre tips available from most graphic suppliers.

Wash lines
As long as you keep the paint wet you can maintain control of it. Draw the border lightly in pencil and then wet the whole area within the pencil lines with clear water prior to painting. Choose a brush the right size for the margin, and start to paint freehand around the mount. Keep going round until the wash line is blended, using clear water to even the paint as you work.

Pen lines
The traditional lining pen used here is versatile because it can be used with both watercolour and ink, and the lines can be thick or thin to suit the image. Mark the line in pencil first, and place a piece of paper at either end to prevent any deposited blobs of colour marking the mount. Use a perspex ruler turned upside down so that the bevels are underneath. This raises it slightly off the mount so that there is no danger of smudging the colour.

Gold paper lines

1 Gold lines are usually fairly thin, so you will either have to cut large sheets into narrow strips or buy thin strips of gold paper, available on rolls from specialist suppliers.

2 Indicate on the mount where the gold paper strip is to be attached. Cut the paper strip to size, and using a 45° angle, cut neat mitres on the paper. It is now ready to be glued onto the mount using paper glue. Gold papers can be given a more "matured" look by painting ink or coloured shellac on top.

Gold acetate

Here a gold line is made with gold leaf pressed onto acetate tape (used, among other things, for heat-stamping gold dates onto leather diaries). Cut the tape to the size of the longer side first, and then you can cut down the same piece for use on the shorter side. Mark the ends of the lines clearly, and use a pointed piece of wood (the end of a small paintbrush is ideal) to score a line. The bright gold side of the tape should be facing you.

Varieties of wash line

1 A double wash line was painted on this mount, with a slightly darker blue on alternate margins. A yellow and black pen line was drawn on the inner sight edge, and the same yellow used again on the outer edge.

2 Circular wash lines are no more difficult to paint than the conventional square or rectangular ones. This example has two pen lines on either side of the wash line, and for these you will need a pen mounted onto a compass, which can either be bought or improvised with a standard compass.

3 A fairly complex design is used for this wash line. The extended corners can add a flourish to the conventional colours and pen lines.

1

2

3

DECORATIVE PAPERS

There are many styles of decorative paper which can be stuck down on mountboard. Some, like the marbled papers, are intensely colourful with dense, intricate patterns, while others are more discreet, with perhaps gold or coloured flecks against a neutral ground. If you go to a specialist supplier you will find hundreds of different types of paper, both hand- and machine-made.

There is no reason why wallpaper should not be used if you can find one of the appropriate pattern and thickness, but in general, you want a thin paper that will not stand out too much from the surface of the mountboard. In recent years there has been a vogue for strips of marbled paper placed around the mounts of prints, particularly botanical album prints and other decorative images. Marbled paper* is thin, and has repeating patterns, so is ideal for this treatment.

Sometimes a whole mount can be covered with a decorative paper, but this can overwhelm the image, so it is more usual to restrict their use to border decorations. They can be used instead of a wash line, or for the inner margins of double and treble mounts where rich decoration in small areas can contrast very well with plain coloured mountboard.

A plain but textured paper, however, can be effective used over the whole mount area. For example good-quality textured, rag watercolour paper glued onto board and then cut to expose the bevels in the window aperture can look very attractive for prints and engravings that only require minimal decoration.

For sharp-edged line decoration in paper it is most important to be neat and accurate. You will need a sharp craft knife, a ruler and a triangular set square with two 45° angles, which will help you cut accurate mitre corners in the paper. These look much neater than simple butt joins.

✱FURTHER INFORMATION

Making marbled
papers   page 63

▶ The photograph shows a small selection of machine-made marbled papers, described as "elephanthide" and "marltone". These are quieter and less obtrusive than the papers shown on page 65, and could be used for a whole mount rather than just as a border.

◄ A wide variety of handmade paper has recently begun to be imported, and these, made from rag or sometimes bark, are available from specialist suppliers at relatively low prices. If you glue heavily textured papers onto board before cutting the mount you will need a strong glue or the paper may lift when the window is cut.

▼ These Japanese papers with gold, silver or coloured strands could look effective used on a mount as long as the image is fairly strong. They are quite thin, so should be stuck on with a water-based wallpaper glue, which will dry without discolouring the paper.

MAKING MARBLED PAPERS

There are two ways to make marbled papers. The first uses oil paint diluted with white spirit, which is floated on a mixture of hot water and gelatine. The second uses a mixture of carragheen moss (seaweed) and water as the base with special marbling inks floated on top. The second method is a demanding and complicated process requiring time and patience, but it yields more intricate and interesting patterns.

Marbling with oil paints is easy to set up and fun to do if you don't mind a bit of mess – children always enjoy it. The moss and inks method, on the other hand, is not suitable for children because the inks are toxic if swallowed even in minute quantities. Special care should be taken to wash hands before eating and drinking.

Carragheen moss can be obtained in its natural state or as a dry concentrated dust. The concentrated powder can be mixed with boiling water directly in the marbling tray. The seaweed should be placed in a saucepan of water (approximately a handful to half a pint of water) and heated until boiling point, then simmered for about half an hour, left overnight and then strained through a fine sieve. It

Oil paint marbling

1 The tank is prepared with hot water and gelatine, using a little more water than you would for making jelly. If the mixture starts to gel add more hot water. If you are using several colours, mix them separately, diluted with white spirit. When the colours are sprinkled onto the surface of the gelatine mixture they should float; if they do not, add more white spirit or a little linseed oil – not too much or it will leave marks on the paper.

2 Combs and other tools can be used to make patterns in the paint. Here a pointed bradawl is used to swirl it around. The thinner the paint, the more easily will it move around.

3 When you have made the pattern, take a piece of paper and carefully place it on the surface of the tank so that it lies flat, then remove it and wash off the excess gelatine under a cold tap. Place the wet papers in between sheets of blotting paper and put some heavy weights on top so that the paper dries flat.

should resemble a soft jelly.

The inks are concentrated and need to be diluted with ox gall (available from artist's suppliers). An exact quantity cannot be given; the only way to know whether you have the right consistency is by experimenting. A drop of colour floated on the seaweed mixture should expand to about 5 cm (2 in) in diameter. If it sinks or is too small, more ox gall is required, or you may need to adjust the seaweed mixture by diluting it with a little more hot water or adding more seaweed.

Once the colours float freely on the tank in circles without mixing together they can be manipulated using combs and other implements.

To take the print you must first treat the paper with alum water, which reduces the glue content and allows the inks to adhere. Mix two tablespoons of alum powder to one pint of hot water, sponge it onto the paper and leave it to dry for a few minutes. The paper should be used just after it has dried; if it is too dry or too wet you will not get a good print.

Seaweed and inks

1 The tank has been prepared with carragheen moss and water mixed to the consistency of thin jelly. This can be thinned further with hot water if necessary. When the colours are dropped onto the surface they should float and expand to 5cm (2in) or more.

2 A variety of implements can be bought or improvised for marbling. Here a comb has been made with thin pins and a piece of wood. The special marbling inks can be manoeuvred in more subtle ways than oil paints, and many intricate patterns can be made. For decorative papers to be used on mounts or frames you want to aim at a repeating effect as opposed to a totally random pattern, and this can be achieved by repeating the movements you make as you manipulate the colours.

3 Before taking a print wet the paper with alum water, allow it to dry a little but not completely and then gently place it on top of the inks. Lift the paper and wash it under a cold tap to remove any excess seaweed, and dry it as for the oil-paint method. Clean the tank between prints by dragging some strips of newspaper across the surface of the tank.

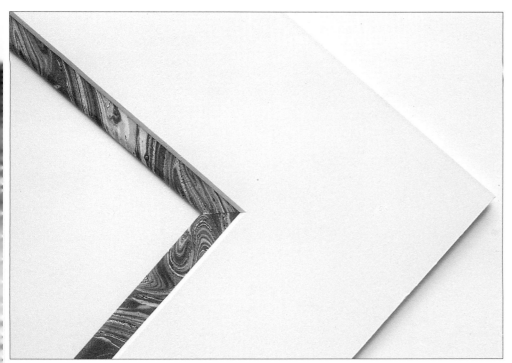

Marbled inner mount

Marbled paper is best used in small quantities, or it could be overpowering. Here the paper has been folded over a deep bevel, which emphasizes the intense patterning. Although the paper is brightly coloured, the visible margin is thin enough to prevent it dominating the picture.

Marbled-paper borders

The marbled paper can also be cut into thin strips and glued onto a mount in place of a wash line. The paper strips should be mitred at the corners for a neater fit. This type of decoration is quite strong, and is often used with prints of flowers and fruit, and other decorative images.

► If you do not have the time and patience to make marbled papers, a large range of both machine-marbled and hand-marbled papers is available from specialist suppliers. These examples are hand made.

FABRIC MOUNTS

Fabric mounts are often used for textiles and embroideries so that there is a physical consistency between the mount and the image. They can also look effective on drawings and paintings. Indian and Persian miniatures were traditionally mounted onto precious silks, with fine fabric seeming to emphasize the jewel-like quality of the paintings themselves.

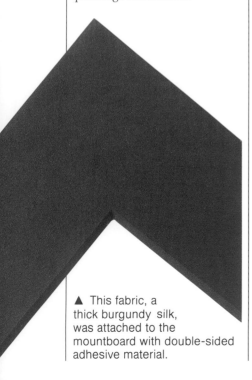

▲ This fabric, a thick burgundy silk, was attached to the mountboard with double-sided adhesive material.

You can obtain fabric-covered mountboards in a variety of colours and thicknesses, but these will, of course, have plain card in the bevels of the window apertures. If you do not like this effect or cannot find a suitable fabric among the manufactured mounts, you can cover plain mountcard with a fabric of your own choice. Some coarser fabrics such as hessian are sometimes painted after they have been attached to the board with a colour chosen to complement the picture. This also slightly reduces the texture.

Fabric can be attached to the board in a number of ways. One is to use dry-mounting tissue, available from photographic suppliers. This is first attached to the board and then the fabric is ironed on. The advantage of this tissue is that it allows you to re-position the fabric if necessary by re-melting the glue with the iron. Other suitable glues are the latex-based fabric glues and the spray-on mounting glues used by graphic designers. Some of the latter also allow for some re-positioning, but read the instructions carefully before you begin.

If you want to emphasize the bevel in a fabric mount, use a double-thickness board or glue two pieces of card together. Great care must be taken to smooth the material so that there are no creases or other imperfections, and to overlap corners and bevels neatly. To prevent any warping of the board as the glue is drying, it is a wise precaution to cover the fabric mount with another board and place some weights on top.

1 The window aperture in the mountcard is cut first. In this example a thick board is used to accentuate the bevels, and the fabric is a thick grey velvet. Place the fabric below the mount, right side down so that the marks will be on the reverse side, and cut it around the mount board, leaving a generous margin.

2 Place the fabric right side down on the mount and mark the dimensions of the window aperture with a soft pencil. Cut out the central piece of fabric with a craft knife. Again, allow a generous margin, so that the fabric can be taken over the bevels.

3 Mark and then cut 45° mitres in each corner of the fabric. Great care must be taken to make these accurate; a little too much and a gap will show and spoil the finish. Before sticking the fabric to the board, it must be ironed to remove all creases.

6 The mount is then placed upside down on the wrong side of the fabric. They are aligned carefully, and the fabric is turned over the bevels and ironed at a low heat. This melts the tissue, so that fabric and board stick together.

4 Thick fabrics can be stuck on with latex glue, but in this case dry-mounting tissue was used. This leaves no marks on the fabric, and allows for re-positioning if necessary. Here it is lightly tacked onto the front surface of the mount using an iron on a low heat.

5 Next the mount is turned over upside down and the flaps of dry-mounting tissue are ironed onto the back of the mount. This ensures that the fabric will adhere to the bevels.

7 Finally, the mount is turned over to the right side, the alignment checked again, and the iron applied to fix the top surface to the mount. A fabric like this velvet could be damaged by heat, so it is protected with a piece of paper.

SPECIAL FINISHES

If you are in any doubt about the presentation of a picture it is always safer to use neutral colours and minimal decoration. However, bolder and more unusual presentations can look effective for some images. The finishes discussed here are stronger than the traditional wash and pen lines*, but do not, of course, have to be used over the entire surface.

Texture

Gesso* can be used to create texture on mounts, stippled for a light texture, or for a heavier one, combed or painted on in patterns or lines. It is important to size the mountboard first with a little glue and leave it to dry before applying the gesso.

Put on four or five coats, waiting only a short time between coats. The glossy wetness should have gone but the gesso should still be damp as you apply the next coat. When you have the required depth of gesso wait a few minutes for it to set before patterning. You will have to work fairly fast, but if the gesso becomes firm before you have finished, apply a further coat and try again.

There is a tendency for the board to warp if too much

moisture is applied, so you may find it more satisfactory to use thicker board or composite board. In any case, it is advisable to weight the board while it is drying.

Gilding

Gold mounts were popular in the late Victorian era, but are less so today. A gold mount is now regarded as too overpowering for most pictures, but a small margin of gold can look very effective, particularly with some decorative images. For example, the inner margin of a double or treble mount* can be gilded so that only a small margin of gold is visible.

The easiest way to gild onto board is to use a water- or oil-based gold size to stick down transfer leaf* or imitation gold*. It is important to size the mount first to render the surface less absorbent. The best effects are obtained by laying one or two coats of burnishing clay under the gold, as in water gilding*, so that any faults will not expose the mount colour, but give the appearance of old gold.

Laying imitation gold
1 First paint on water-based gold size, making sure that the brushmarks are blended into a smooth surface. In this case the bevel is to be gilded as well, so a window aperture has been cut first.

2 After fifteen minutes the size will be dry enough for the gold leaf to be applied. This is imitation gold which, unlike real gold leaf, can be picked up with the fingers and cut to size with scissors.

3 Apply the second leaf next to the first, and work methodically around the mount. The leaf will only stick where there is some glue.

4 Smooth down each piece of leaf with tissue paper taken from the book of leaf. To prevent tarnishing, the leaf must be lacquered.

BROKEN COLOUR EFFECTS

Water-based colours sponged onto the surface of the mount can look effective, but care must be taken not to put too much water onto the board, as this can cause warping, and also the top paper, which is only glued down, may start to cockle and lift.

Several colours can be used, or you can restrict yourself to one, and use the board itself as a second colour. Paint can also be spattered and sprayed onto the mount surface, and you can achieve a wide variety of effects. Spraying with an airbrush will produce a delicate colour wash formed by an almost imperceptible screen of coloured dots, while for a slightly bolder effect, watercolour can be flicked on with a toothbrush or an artist's bristle brush.

Spattering is a messy process, so if you only want a margin of spattered colour you will have to mask the areas to be kept clean. Most adhesive tapes tend to damage mountboard, so the best way to mask the mount is to cut a window in a piece of card the same length and width as the margin you wish to spatter.

Spattering

1 Some crimson gouache paint was mixed as the first colour. The paint needs to be well diluted with water so that the drops of colour fall easily from the brush as it is knocked against the stick.

2 Blue gouache paint was then spattered over the red. Both brilliant and subtle colours can be achieved in this way, with the colour of the mountboard contributing to the overall effect.

Sponging

1 Again, water-based paint is used, mixed with a little glue to give it more body.

2 Water is dropped onto the surface of the colour to keep it moist.

3 While still wet, the colour is sponged again to increase the density of the pattern.

CHAPTER 5

WOOD AND WOOD FINISHES

There are a great many attractive woods, most of which are suitable for picture framing, but unfortunately you will find only a small selection are in ready made moulding form. A good reason for investing in a router or combination plane is that you can make up original moulding designs with any wood that is available. Those most commonly used by framemakers are listed on the next page, but there are other indigenous woods, which vary from country to country, such as fruitwoods, which are equally suitable for frames. There is also the possibility of using veneers; some of the rarer woods, and those with particularly attractive grains and patterns, are only available in veneer form.

Endangered woods
Nowadays there are ecological considerations involved in the choice of wood. The more widely available woods such as pine, ash and oak are generally considered to come from sustainable forests in Europe and North America, and are thus ecologically sound, but other popular woods, among them ramin, obeche and mahogany, come from forests in South East Asia, Africa and South America, which are not usually sustainable. Unfortunately these tropical hardwoods are used extensively in the manufacture of frames and mouldings, which makes it difficult to avoid them – many mouldings are only available in these woods. It is to be hoped, however, that refusing to buy such timber will eventually persuade the manufacturers to cease importing tropical hardwoods.

VARIETIES OF WOOD

The woods most commonly used by professional picture framers are pine, ash, oak, ramin, obeche and mahogany. Pine is a soft wood, and is more prone to shrinkage and general damage than the hardwoods. It has a clearly defined grain, and the poorer-quality pine is often studded with knots. However, it is cheap, widely available and easy to cut, and is thus much used for framemaking. The surface is usually stained* or painted* to disguise the paleness of the wood, though it does not have to be.

Ash and oak are both durable hardwoods, and are quite similar, though oak is usually darker. Both have attractive grains which makes them ideal for frames with a natural wood finish, but they are also suitable for staining, oiling, liming* and painting. They are more expensive than some other hardwoods and almost twice the price of pine.

Ramin comes from South East Asia, and is probably the most frequently used hardwood in picture framing at the present time. It has a pale creamy brown colour and a very close, even grain. This and its hardness allows mouldings to be cut more finely than they can in soft pine, so it is often used for the more detailed design profiles.

Obeche comes from West Africa and is a soft, light and somewhat featureless wood rather similar to balsa wood. Because of its lightness, it is useful for making wide-sectioned mouldings. Mahogany, most of which comes from Brazil, is medium textured with a straight grain and a reddish-brown colour. It is softer than most hardwoods and has an attractive finish.

*FURTHER INFORMATION

Wood stains	page 76
Paint finishes	pages 82-107
Liming	page 74

◄ Wood veneers
Veneers are useful for natural wood finishes where you want a more exotic look than the standard pine, oak or ramin. They can only be used on flat or gently curved mouldings, however.
1 Castello
2 Bird's eye maple
3 European walnut
4 Plane
5 Rosewood
6 Ash

▼ The russet colours of the fox and winter woodland are picked up in the rich-coloured burr veneer moulding. The print, "Red Fox", is by Carl Brenders, and the frame by Stephen and Linda Hible of Right Angle Picture Framing.

▲ These two frames were made by Stephen Field for portrait photographs. They are veneered in amboyna with boxwood lines (left) and yew with rosewood lines (right), and both are decorated with elegant fan inlays.

▶ There are many native European soft and hard woods which can be used for making frames and furniture. These range in colour and pattern from the pale sycamore and ash to the more colourful yew and fruitwoods.

1 Sycamore
2 Ash
3 Oak
4 Ash
5 Beech
6 Acacia
7 Pine
8 Cherry
9 Yew

LIMING

Limed wood, popular in the 1920s and 30s, is now enjoying a revival. It involves "pushing" white pigment into the wood grain, which gives a subtle emphasis to the pattern of the wood. Ash or oak are the woods most often chosen for this treatment, as their grain holds the white pigment well.

The grain can be made deeper by lightly scorching the surface, which burns out the softer wood to provide a deeper relief. This method is only suitable for ash and oak. Mature pine has a raised grain – you can often see this on old floorboards. To artificially deepen the grain of new pine, the wood must first be softened by wrapping wet rags around it and leaving for a day or overnight. The wood can then be scratched into with a steel brush, leaving score marks which follow the grain of the wood.

For the liming process itself you can use either gesso* or liming wax. Gesso can be made more intensely white by adding titanium white pigment to the mixture. Liming wax can be bought ready made, but can also be mixed by adding titanium white to clear wax.

If gesso is used, warm it before application, and apply one or two coats with a brush so that all the grain is covered. When it is dry, wipe off the excess with a damp cloth.

With liming wax it is advisable to seal the wood first with a thin coat of shellac. When the shellac is dry rub the liming wax into the wood with fine steel wool to fill the grain, then rub on some clear wax to remove the excess white, and finally polish with a soft clean cloth.

Liming wax is rather more difficult to rub off than gesso, and tends to leave a white bloom over the whole surface of the wood. This residue can look attractive with certain pictures, but it can be removed with white spirit.

✽FURTHER INFORMATION

Recipe for gesso   page 111

Scorching
A flat profile in oak is scorched using a plumber's blowtorch. Sweep the flame to and fro over each piece of the frame, being careful not to concentrate on any one area for too long. The rebate, being the thinnest part of the frame, is particularly vulnerable to burning.

Liming over scorched wood
A liming wax is rubbed in with grade 0000 steel wool, which forces the white wax deep into the grain. The excess white wax is then cleaned off using either clear wax or white spirit. Here the scorched and limed wood is seen next to the plain one. On the limed section you can see the darker burnt wood as well as the limed grain.

Liming plain wood

1 For a paler effect, simply rub the liming wax onto plain wood, allow it to dry and then rub in some clear wax, which will take off most of the excess.

Liming with gesso

The traditional method of liming is to paint gesso onto wood, usually oak or ash. For greater contrast titanium white pigment can be added to the gesso mixture. One or two coats are usually sufficient to fill the grain. Allow the gesso to dry, and then wipe over the frame with a damp cloth or sponge, which helps to dissolve the glue in the gesso. The wood grain will be white, but the rest of the timber will be clean.

2 In this method a bloom of white is left over the whole surface. This can look attractive, but if not wanted it can be removed using white spirit.

► These four samples show how the three liming methods differ. The plain oak is shown at the bottom, with the gesso over scorched wood above it. Next is the plain timber with white wax, and at the top white wax over scorched wood. Liming presents many possibilities, as you do not have to use white; other colours can be pushed into the grain.

STAINING AND COLOURING

In some cases a clear finish is suitable for a frame, but often a stain is used, either to complement a colour in the picture or to enhance the natural grain and colour of the wood. Before staining the frame must be clean, and should be sanded down to a smooth finish.

There are three types of wood stain: oil, spirit and water-based. Oil-based stains, available ready mixed in a wide range of colours from most large hardware stores, are easy to apply, and can be thinned – or removed completely – with white spirit.

Spirit-based stains are aniline dyes, which can be bought in powder form from specialist suppliers and mixed with methylated spirits. There is a large range of colours available, including bright primaries, and they can be mixed together to obtain the exact shade you require. Methylated spirits evaporates quickly, which can result in uneven colouring, but this can be remedied by rubbing with steel wool and a little methylated spirits until an even spread of colour is obtained. The powders can also be added to shellac* to make a coloured polish.

Water stains are also aniline dyes, but in this case they are, of course, water-soluble. They are available either in powder form or ready mixed, are easy to apply and can be thinned with water.

All stains can be applied with either a brush or a rag, and the edges of the stain should be blended as quickly as possible. Protective gloves should be worn when applying wood stain.

✽FURTHER INFORMATION

Shellac, see under Waxes
    and polishes   page 81

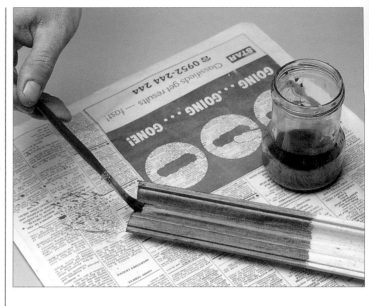

▲ **Spirit stains**
These aniline dye stains are very concentrated, so they need to be mixed with a lot of methylated spirits. Mix the stain thoroughly and test the colour on the back of the frame or a spare piece of wood before applying it. The stain can either be brushed on or rubbed on with a cloth. If you rub it in, use protective gloves, as it is difficult to wipe off hands.

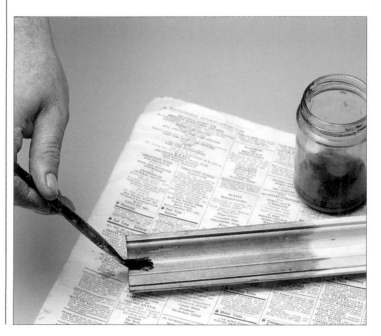

◄ **Water stains**
These are the same as spirit stains, except that the dyes are mixed with water rather than alcohol. There is a tendency for the water to lift the grain of the wood slightly, but when dry the frame can be rubbed smooth and then varnished and waxed.

▲ These have been coloured with either water or spirit stains. Interesting colour variations can be obtained by mixing and diluting the stains. The colours separate in a similar way to inks as they are diluted, for example the black spirit stain turns an attractive purple-grey when thinned with methylated spirits. Water and spirit stains are not compatible with one another and do not mix well with mineral colour pigments.

- Water-based stain (dye)
- Water-based stain
- Spirit stain
- Dye powder
- Dye powder
- Dye powder
- Shellac

FUMED WOOD

Fuming is a process of colouring wood by exposing it to the fumes of ammonia. The depth of colour can be controlled by the length of exposure.

You will need an airtight "fume tent", which you can make by covering a light wooden frame with black plastic and sealing the joins of the plastic with tape. When using ammonia, wear goggles and a face mask. Put the frame inside the tent with some saucers containing ammonia, leave for a day and then check the colour. If a darker colour is required leave the frame in the tent, checking from time to time.

Plastic cover
Adhesive tape
Wooden framework
Saucers of ammonia
Baseboard
Frame

▶ These two corners of oak moulding show the difference between the natural wood and the fumed wood, which in this case was left in a fume cupboard with a saucer of strong ammonia for twenty-four hours. Diluted household ammonia can be used, but will take much longer to colour the wood.

WOOD GRAINING

Imitation wood graining is a method which has been practised for many years. It was particularly popular in the Victorian era, when pine furniture and the fittings of urban houses were made to look like oak.

The most widely used method of wood graining is to use an oil-and-driers medium known as a scumble glaze* over a biscuit-coloured undercoat or, for exotic finishes such as ebony, maple, satinwood and tulipwood, a smooth gesso undercoat. Scumble glazes are available from fine-art suppliers or decorative-paint stores, either in their basic transparent form or ready mixed in a wide range of wood colours. For a special colour, you can mix your own using artist's oil colours.

A wide selection of tools and brushes has been devised for the graining itself. These include steel and rubber combs and rockers for simulating the pattern of wood graining and blending brushes for brush graining; stippling brushes and feathers for backgrounds.

When attempting any imitation effect, whether wood grain or precious stone, it is essential to have adequate visual reference, either a small sample of the actual material,

or a good photograph. If you try to work from memory you will almost certainly make the pattern too repetitive; in nature there is always a subtle non-conformity.

The fascination of rare and exotic woods lies in their depth of colour, patterns and smooth surface, and to simulate these effects in paint it is essential to keep the surface equally smooth and even. This is done by keeping the paint film to a minimum and rubbing down with fine abrasives when the paint is dry.

*FURTHER INFORMATION

Paints, varnishes and mediums   page 86

2 The frame has been gessoed, smoothed down and then painted with an ochre shellac undercoat. The first oil colours are now stippled on.

The colours used are raw umber, burnt umber, raw sienna and burnt sienna.

1 The paints used for the first stage are oil colours. Here a scumble glaze, which keeps the paints wet and easy to manipulate, is mixed with liquid driers and white spirit to speed up the drying time.

3 The brush is charged with glaze before some colour is picked up (burnt and raw umber), and dabbed onto the frame in a deliberately haphazard way. The two sienna colours are applied in the same way and the process is repeated.

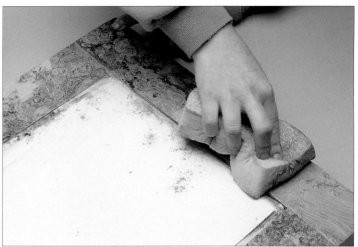

4 To simulate the effect of a butt joint, a piece of sandpaper is used face down as a barrier, and excess colour is wiped off one side of the frame. The sandpaper will not smudge the wet oil colour.

7 The Fuller's earth is then wiped off with a sponge and water. In this picture you can see the effect of the simulated butt joint very clearly. This is the traditional way of joining a wood veneer.

5 The wood grain effect is built up slowly and gradually, with cotton buds, old pencils and brushes used to take off and add colour in a circular motion. At this stage, the colour is left to dry overnight.

6 When the oil colour is dry, Fuller's earth (or finely ground chalk) is sprinkled onto the surface. This process, known as "cissing", reduces the oil and helps the top colours to adhere.

8 The top colour now being used is water-based, and so it is necessary to make a binder or it will not adhere to the lower layer of oil. In this case one part vinegar to three parts water is used.

9 The water-based paint, crystals of Vandyke brown soaked overnight in water, is applied with a large brush charged with binder and colour.

10 The same brush, a camel hair "cutter" brush, is rocked and moved up and down to mottle and wave the surface.

11 Finally, the top colour needs to be "strapped down" using an oil-based eggshell varnish, thinned with white spirit on the first coat. Wood graining is a slow process, but in this case has produced a marvellously convincing impression of burr walnut.

▶ Walnut grain
These samples, of a different type of walnut, were painted in the same way as the frame, starting with oil colours on top of an ochre undercoat. The distinctive grain markings were made by dragging a rubber rocker through the wet oil paint, and watercolour was later added to give more light to the pattern. The demonstration and the samples were done by Louise Taylor.

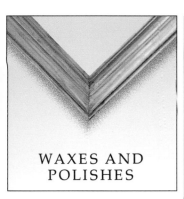

WAXES AND POLISHES

There are four main categories of finishes applied to raw wood: wax, shellac, lacquer and varnish, and oil.

Wax gives an attractive eggshell finish and is very simple to apply, requiring no equipment other than a rag. There are many types of wax polish, but the beeswax-based ones are most often used for wood. If you want to add a touch of colour to pale wood you can mix powder pigment with clear wax, or use one of the ready mixed colour waxes that correspond to different wood colours.

Shellac, a varnish made from the secretion of an insect (the lac), goes under many different names, including French polish and button polish. It is sold ready mixed in bottles or as flakes which can be mixed in alcohol.

It can be applied either with a brush or with a French polishing "rubber", which is simply a square of linen wrapped round a piece of cotton wadding which has first been soaked with shellac. A little linseed oil is used as a lubricant.

If you apply shellac with a brush you can put on several coats in a short time; a new coat can be applied as soon as the first is "touch-dry". You must leave it longer than this before sanding, however – a minimum of two hours – as it will still be tacky underneath.

Shellac is a versatile polish, and can be mixed with aniline spirit dyes* and pigments to make coloured polishes as well. Its only disadvantage is that it is not very water- or heat-resistant and so should not be used for frames to be hung in a bathroom or kitchen.

Cellulose lacquers and varnishes are very hard, damp-proof and heat-resistant. They are also very quick drying, and when used industrially are usually applied with a spray-gun, though a brush can also be used. Pre-catalysed plastic lacquers have similar characteristics. They will give a durable high gloss finish. Make sure that they are compatible with any paints or stains underneath. They react badly to oily surfaces.

Modern wood varnishes such as polyurethane* are also extremely hard-wearing and water- and heat-resistant. They take twelve hours or more to dry, and should be sanded down between coats.

Oils, usually Danish oil and Tung oil, are traditionally used on oily woods such as teak which resist other finishes, but they can also be used effectively on other hardwoods and softwoods. Oil nourishes and protects wood and leaves an attractive natural appearance. You will need to apply three or four coats allowing six hours drying time between the first two coats and twenty-four hours for any subsequent ones.

*FURTHER INFORMATION

Wood stains   page 78
Paints, mediums
    and varnishes   page 86

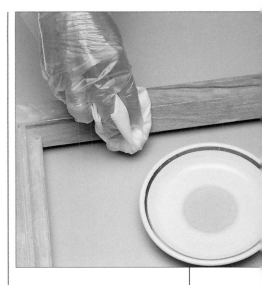

Shellac
Here shellac is applied with a home-made version of the French-polishing "rubber". This is simply a wad of cotton wool dipped in shellac and wrapped in a rag.

Wax
Wax is quickly and easily applied with a rag. Progressive applications over a period of time will build up a rich glow without substantially changing the colour of the wood.

Oil
Danish oil imparts a rich golden colour. If the grain becomes raised and rough when using either oil or shellac, rub down with wire wool between coats.

CHAPTER 6

PAINT FINISHES

An ever-increasing range of pre-decorated picture frame mouldings is available today, with many elaborate and attractive finishes in both modern and traditional designs. You may find that your requirements are adequately catered for by moulding manufacturers, but many people still prefer hand-finished frames, with shapes, colours and textures chosen for individual pictures.

The more delicate and refined finishes, such as water gilding and colour washes over gesso, can seldom be supplied by moulding manufacturers, mainly because these finishes are fragile, and would require careful transport and storage as well as many layers of protective lacquer. The latter would in many cases destroy the effect, as the beauty of hand-finished frames often lies in their unvarnished surface and the original designs of the framer.

Decorative paint finishes are usually applied after the frame has been assembled, with the finish painted over the mitred corners to give a neater, more attractive appearance.

UNDERCOATING

Before applying a paint finish, absorbent surfaces are usually treated with some form of size. This can be animal-skin glue or PVA (polyvinyl acetate)* thinned with a little water. Whichever you use, allow it to dry before applying paint. To achieve a smooth top surface, the next step is to put some undercoats onto the frame, thus forming a good base to hold the subsequent layers of paint. Ordinary household emulsions or oil paints can be used as undercoats as long as they are compatible with the paint that is to be used on top.

Gesso*, important in the gilding process, is also used as an undercoat for painted finishes. It is normally made from whiting and rabbit-skin glue, but can also be made with casein (see recipe). The advantage of casein gesso is that it can be stored and used cold, unlike skin-glue gesso which has to be heated.

✳FURTHER INFORMATION

Paints, mediums and varnishes	page 86
Recipe for gesso	page 111

Texture
1 Some paint finishes are improved by an underlying texture. You can make a variety of raised patterns in thick gesso or wet plaster by combing, stippling or pressing a rough fabric into the surface.

Preparation
To prime the wood and provide a smooth, well-sealed surface for a paint finish you can use household oil undercoats, emulsion paints or acrylic gesso, depending on the type of paint to be used on top.

2 Here a thin wash of water-based paint is applied over the combed-gesso texture.

3 A damp sponge is lightly drawn over the surface, removing some of the paint from the ridges to highlight the effect.

4 The first colour has been allowed to dry, and a darker one laid on top. The finished frame can be seen on page 162.

RECIPE FOR CASEIN SIZE AND GESSO

Ingredients
- Powdered casein 2 parts
- Water 16 parts
- Ammonium carbonate (powdered) 1 part
- Whiting

Method
Use fresh casein if possible, because it loses its strength with time. Mix it into half the water, stirring to get rid of any lumps.

For gesso, simply add sufficient whiting to the casein solution to make a creamy consistency. If it does not seem smooth, strain it through muslin or a fine sieve.

Add the ammonium carbonate, stir again, and leave to stand for one hour before adding the remaining water. This mixture can be used as a size or as a vehicle for paint or gesso.

To make paint, add finely ground pigments to the casein and a little water to thin if required.

PAINTS, MEDIUMS, AND VARNISHES

Because there are so many types of paint and varnish available, this summary may provide a useful reference. Remember that it is important to handle paints and varnishes with care. The mineral pigments used in most paints are poisonous and many of the solvents are highly toxic. Work in a well-ventilated room, avoid eating or drinking while you work, and wear protective clothing if you are using toxic substances. Gloves, goggles and masks are available from most do-it-yourself and ironmongery shops.

PAINTS

Types	Composition	Uses
Acrylic (artist's)	Finely ground pigments in water-soluble acrylic base	A strong solid matt paint. When thinned, it is suitable for washes. Water-resistant when dry
Gouache and poster colour	Pigments mixed with gum arabic or synthetic compounds. Additional filler makes gouache more opaque than watercolour	A thick opaque watercolour with a flat matt finish
Oil colour (artist's)	Pigments finely ground in oil, usually linseed or poppy	Comprehensive colour range. Can be thinned for colour washes, and suspended in mediums for glazes. Strong colour
Egg tempera	Finely ground pigment in an egg-yolk and water medium	An attractive paint for thin colour washes, can also be used for denser colour effects
Watercolour (artist's)	Finely ground pigments mixed with gum arabic and other binders	Good for translucent colour washes and for tinting over gold and silver
Decorator's emulsion	Synthetic resins and pigments	Available in a wide range of colours and finishes. It can be diluted for use as a wash. Also useful as an undercoat. Water-resistant when dry
Decorator's oil-based paint	Pigments and synthetic compounds	A thick, durable paint, available in many colours and finishes

MEDIUMS AND VARNISHES

Casein	Casein (substance made from the curd of milk). Bought in powder form and mixed with ammonium carbonate and water	Used as a glue, size, or as a medium to make a durable and thick paint with an attractive velvet matt finish. Water-resistant when dry
PVA (Polyvinyl acetate)	Colourless resin used in emulsion paints and glues	A useful glue and, in thinned form, paint medium. Water-resistant when dry
Transparent oil glaze ("scumble")	Oil- and resin-based medium with driers	Very useful as a paint medium for marbling woodgraining and other paint finishes
Acrylic varnish	Acrylic resin in petroleum solvent (also water-based version)	Colourless varnish that dries to a satin finish
Polyurethane varnish	Synthetic resins and oil base	Widely available household varnish. Suitable for all decorative finishes, but tends to yellow with age
Shellac (french polish)	Insect deposits suspended in alcohol	Useful as a medium for colour lacquers, as a varnish, and as an isolating layer between films of paint
Damar and mastic varnishes	Naturally occurring resins suspended in oil	Clear varnishes for oil-based paints. Long lasting with good protective properties

Solvents	Drying time and other peculiarities
Water	Touch dry in 5–10 minutes. Good covering power, but expensive for large areas
Water	Touch dry in a few minutes. A traditional thick watercolour, useful for precise paintwork. Good covering power
Turpentine or white spirit	Touch dry in 24 hours, but longer final drying time. Can be made to dry more quickly with Alkyd and other driers. Useful for many paint effects
Water	Touch dry in a few minutes, but takes longer to fully dry. More difficult to use than some other water-based paints. Also used for sgraffito over gold
Water	Touch dry in a few minutes. Must be varnished or waxed, because it remains water-soluble when dry and is therefore vulnerable
Water	Quick drying decorator's paint (1–3 hours). Inexpensive and available at most local shops. Good covering power
Turpentine or white spirit	Slow drying (6–12 hours). More often used on large areas. Needs a primer and undercoat for an effective finish
Water	A form of gesso can be made with casein size. Good for building up layers of undercoat. Touch dry in 10–20 minutes
Water	Touch dry in approximately 20 minutes. Also useful as a size, sealer and varnish
Turpentine or white spirit	A flexible medium that allows manipulation with feathers, combs and rags for 30 minutes. Dry in approximately 6 hours
Water	Touch dry in approximately 1 hour. Easy to use, an all purpose decorator's varnish
Turpentine or white spirit	Dry in 6–12 hours. A tough varnish available in matt, silk and gloss finishes
Methylated spirits	Touch dry in 5–10 minutes, but must not be rubbed down for 2 hours after application
Turpentine or white spirit	Slow drying time: approximately 24 hours. An attractive gloss finish

COLOUR WASHES

Although there are so many different types of paint, they can be divided into two broad categories – transparent and opaque. A thin paint lying over a lighter ground will appear transparent because light is reflected back through the top layer from the light background. When, on the other hand, the coat of paint lies on a background of the same colour or a darker one the background does not reflect light, and the effect is called opaque.

Laying transparent colour washes, either with oil or watercolour paints, is a technique which has been practised by artists and decorators for centuries. For maximum luminosity a white ground is used, which could be either white paint or gesso. The system of painting one colour over another creates greater variations of depth of tone than one single coat, and can produce very beautiful colour harmonies.

Colour lacquers, similarly, are usually built up layer by layer on a smooth ground – the more layers you use, the less transparent the effect.

Lacquers can be made by putting dry pigment or aniline dyes* into shellac*, which dries very quickly – in five to ten minutes – allowing you to build up several layers in a short time. However, even when "touch-dry" the shellac will still remain tacky underneath, so allow two hours drying time before rubbing down. If you want a high gloss, rub down only every two or three coats and the penultimate one with a light abrasive such as "wet-and-dry" paper or grade 0000 steel wool. For an eggshell finish you can use the same abrasives, but rub each coat before the final one, and for a matt finish the last coat can also be rubbed down.

✳FURTHER INFORMATION

Waxes and polishes   page 81

1 Before a colour wash is applied, the frame should be prepared with gesso and sanded to a smooth finish. The gesso is then given a coat of rabbit-skin size to make it less absorbent and ensure an even spread of colour. With the size now dry, the first colour, an indigo blue, is painted onto the central margin.

2 The next colour, a mixture of burnt sienna and yellow ochre, is painted onto the sides and outer edge. Choose a brush of appropriate shape and size for the area being painted so that it can be easily brushed along the margin. If a darker tone is required another coat can be applied as soon as the first one has dried.

3 To soften or remove the colours in places a damp sponge can be wiped around the frame, which will also even out any overlapping brushstrokes. Here the sponge is used to remove colour from the high outside edge, emphasizing the moulding profile.

4 Finally, a mixture of yellow and yellow ochre is painted onto the sight edge margin to echo the colour of the outside edge. Many colour combinations can be tried, chosen to harmonize with the picture, and modified with water for subtle variations.

▶ The light blue and brown used in the painting were repeated on the frame. Watercolour paints were used, protected with a layer of clear wax.

▶ Bright colours were painted onto a gesso ground with watercolour and then washed off the ridges. When dry, the frame was waxed with a dark brown wax to soften the colours.

DISTRESSED PAINT EFFECTS

The passage of time and the general effects of wear and tear give a mature and subtle patina to old painted frames, and this ageing is often simulated on new ones to impart a richer colour and softer appearance.

Distressing a paint surface is done by rubbing off some of the top layer of paint, thus exposing the undercoat, something which occurs naturally with age. Oriental laquerware (*Negoro nuri*), for example, was first lacquered in black and then in red. As the top layer was repeatedly polished the black undercoat began to show through, enhancing the rich appearance.

First apply two or three coats of undercolour. The underpainting must be strong enough to remain undamaged when abrasives are applied to the top coat. This top layer needs to be densely coloured but not too thick, as it is obviously easier to rub off a thin coat of paint.

All the paint must be dry before rubbing down, or the abrasives will stick and leave unsightly rucks in the surface. Either water- or oil-based paints can be used or they can be combined, in which case the water-based colour must lie beneath the oil.

Water-based paint

1 Ordinary emulsion paint or artist's acrylics can be used for the first coat. Here two coats of red emulsion have been applied over a surface prepared with gesso. When dry, a coat of green was applied on top, allowed to dry in turn and then lightly rubbed with wire wool.

2 Fine sandpaper, which is more abrasive than wire wool, is now used to remove more of the green top coat. Care must be taken not to rub too hard or to use too coarse a grade of sandpaper, or the lower layer of paint will also begin to come off.

Burnishing clay

1 A terracotta burnishing clay over a gesso ground was used as an undercoat, and to make this thick and strong three coats were painted on. When the top coat is distressed by rubbing with an abrasive, the undercoat must remain solid. The top coat in this case is black clay, applied over the red base coat.

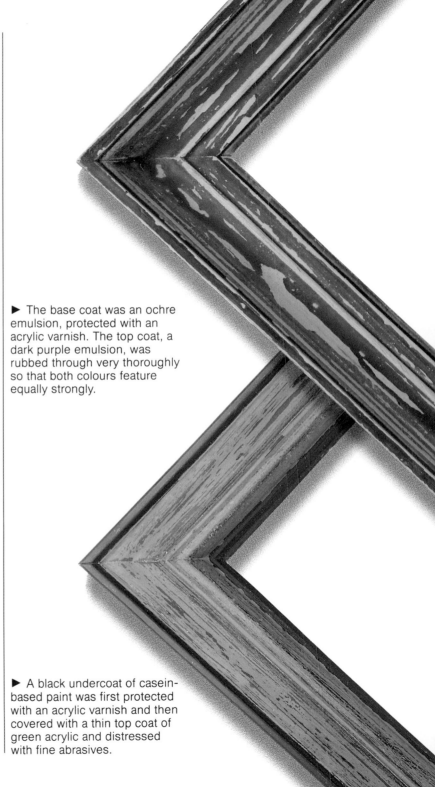

▶ The base coat was an ochre emulsion, protected with an acrylic varnish. The top coat, a dark purple emulsion, was rubbed through very thoroughly so that both colours feature equally strongly.

2 When the top coat is dry it can be rubbed with either grade 0000 steel wool or a fine wet-and-dry abrasive paper, which will partially remove the black to reveal the red beneath.

Other types of paint can be distressed in a similar manner, sometimes using a solvent as well as an abrasive for the top coat.

▶ A black undercoat of casein-based paint was first protected with an acrylic varnish and then covered with a thin top coat of green acrylic and distressed with fine abrasives.

CRACKLE FINISHES

In principle, putting a slow-drying paint or varnish below a faster-drying one should be avoided. Paint or varnish shrinks slightly as it dries, and as the slow-drying lower layer contracts it will cause cracks in the dry upper one. However, these small cracks on a surface can be attractive, and are sometimes deliberately induced by applying a glaze of gum arabic and ox gall over an oil-based varnish.

The timing between the two coats is critical, as by varying the drying times you can control the size of the cracks. They will in any case be very fine, so the effect is usually emphasized by rubbing in a colour, usually an oil paint.

Another type of crackle agent is a transparent water-based glaze called Pervolac, produced for the film industry to create instant cracked-paint effects. To be effective, Pervolac needs to be sandwiched between two layers of emulsion or other water-based paints. For this type of crackle glaze, it is best to apply the top coat of emulsion paint with an airbrush rather than a bristle brush, which can cause rucking in the soft glaze.

Varnish crackle
1 The paint or gesso surface should be rubbed smooth before the application of the crackle glazes. Here gesso is used as a base coat, and has been sealed to make it less absorbent. You can use either size or shellac varnish. The oil-based varnish, with added colour for an ageing effect, is then painted evenly over the surface.

2 The water-based varnish is painted on top when the oil varnish is still moist but not tacky. The brand used here, called Crackleur, needs twenty to thirty minutes. The length of time between each application determines the extent of the cracking. You may need to experiment, as varnishes react to atmospheric conditions.

3 To emphasize the cracks, which are practically invisible on their own, a little umber oil paint has been rubbed over the frame. The underlying varnish takes some time to dry and cause the cracking. This could be anything from a few hours to a few days depending on atmospheric conditions and the thickness of the lower layer of varnish.

4 The water-based top glaze is vulnerable to damp, so it is wise to protect the finish with a wax or a varnish. Wait until the cil paint or ink in the cracks is dry before applying the top protection.

Pervolac
1 Pervolac is a thick water-based glaze designed to be used with an airbrush, but it can also be applied with a soft paintbrush. Here it is painted over a black emulsion basecoat. It is important to paint an even covering in order to achieve cracks of the same dimension.

USING GOLD

Many variations of colour and paint can be tried for both the base coat and the cracks. In this example, varnish was painted on top of red burnishing clay, water glaze was applied on top, and gold wax was then rubbed into the cracks.

2 When the Pervolac has gelled but not hardened (approximately ten to twenty minutes) apply the top coat of paint. In this case the top coat is white emulsion, chosen to create a dramatic black-crack effect. Be careful with brushstrokes on the top layer, because too much pressure will break the weak skin of the glaze.

Pervolac with an airbrush

1 Again, Pervolac was brushed over a black basecoat, and a yellow emulsion is now sprayed on top with an airbrush. Colours can be mixed with a suitable water medium such as acrylic, PVA, or emulsion paint, but must not be too thick or they will be difficult to spray. The emulsion is sprayed on with a back-and-forth motion to provide an even coating all over the frame. The top layer of paint begins to crack almost immediately.

▲ The frame was first coated with black oil paint, and then "crackleur" varnish was applied. This comes in two parts, an oil varnish, which is used first, and a water-based one; the action of the two forms the cracks.

2 Different patterns of cracking can be achieved by varying the texture of the paint. Thicker paint will give broader cracks, while the thin, diluted emulsion used in this example gives close, delicate cracks. The airbrush also allows you to experiment with the drying time of the Pervolac glaze.

► In this case, dark red paint mixed with shellac was applied before the "crackleur" varnish. Pale green paint was rubbed in to emphasize the cracks; this appears almost white against the rich deep red.

EGGSHELL INLAY

An attractive and unusual surface can be created by glueing eggshells onto a ground and then grouting in the cracks. This gives a mosaic-like effect, which can be either painted, gilded or left as a natural colour and varnished.

The eggshells must first be soaked in a solution of household bleach (sodium hypochlorite), for at least two days. This breaks down the membranes of the shell and makes it easier to stick them onto the frame — as well as removing any residue of egg white. PVA glue is painted onto the surface of the frame and the pieces of eggshell are pressed into place.

When the glue is dry a grout is rubbed between the cracks to create a smooth surface, after which the eggshell can be rubbed down with fine wet-and-dry paper and varnished.

1 After bleaching for two days and rinsing in vinegar and water, the eggshells are ready to stick down. The frame should be smooth and sealed with a glue or a varnish. To stick the eggshell, simply apply PVA glue to a small part of the frame and press each one into place. Continue working section by section.

2 The long sides of the eggshell are easier to press because they are flatter than the more sharply curved top edges. Press the eggshell until it cracks and lies flat against the frame. It is obviously easier to do this over a flat or gently curved moulding profile.

3 When all the spaces have been filled and the glue is dry, the cracks are filled in with grout. Proprietary brands of floor- and wall-tile grout, which are available in both white and a range of colours, can be used for this. If you are unable to find a suitable colour, you can mix white grout with dry pigments. Wipe all excess grout off the eggshell before it dries.

4 In this example a dark grey grout was used as a contrast to the natural colour of the eggshells. When the grout is dry the whole surface can be rubbed smooth with various grades of wet-and-dry paper, wiped clean with a damp cloth and then protected and enhanced with coats of varnish, shellac or wax.

MARBLE AND LAPIS LAZULI

Painted imitation marble has a long history, and various ingenious methods of simulating its grain have been devised. Semi-precious stones such as lapis lazuli can also be imitated on frames.

Either water- or oil-based paints can be used for these finishes, but oil paint is easier to use, as its slow-drying quality allows more time to create the effect you want. A useful medium for all decorative work with oil paint is scumble glaze*, made with linseed oil and driers. When mixed with oil paint, the additional oil provides flexibility, while the driers cut down the drying time.

The background colour may feature in the final surface, so it should be chosen carefully. It is important to begin with a firm undercoat and then protect it with shellac or varnish, which enables you to experiment with the top layers of paint without disturbing the base coat.

*FURTHER INFORMATION

Paints, mediums
and varnishes   page 86

Marble

1 A fine smooth ground is essential for any imitation-stone finish. In this case a gesso surface was rubbed smooth and sealed with rabbit-skin size. Artist's oil paints – ochre and burnt sienna – were mixed with scumble glaze, and are now stippled onto the frame.

2 To make the background texture pattern, the paint is dabbed on with a rag. The film of paint is thin enough to allow the luminosity of the brilliant white gesso to show through. This finish simulates Sienese marble, in which some white is usually visible, and this effect is best achieved by exposing the white gesso in places.

3 Delicate patterning and subtle blends of colour can be achieved with a feather dipped in white spirit. Here the feather is used as a brush to paint the black veins typical of this type of marble. Some white gesso is exposed within the veins. When the oil paint is dry it can be lightly rubbed down and then varnished or waxed for extra protection.

▲ This composite marble frame made by Isabella Kocum is reminiscent of the tabletops of marble and semi-precious gem stones made in Renaissance times. The individual shapes of the patterned stones were drawn out and engraved on gesso.

► The distinctive grey and white markings of Sicilian marble have been imitated on the frame at the top. The finish was painted with scumble glaze mixed with oil paint, and the veining was done with a feather and blending brushes. The other frame (right), also marbled, has gilt corner ornaments in pastiglia (see page 120). The marbling was done in the same way, but in this case the white markings were achieved by exposing the gesso undercoat. Both frames were made by Isabella Kocum.

3 The colours should be wet with scumble glaze, so that they can be manipulated to form convincing patterns.

Lapis lazuli
1 The surface should be painted with gesso or undercoat and sanded smooth. Two or more black basecoats are then applied, followed by a coat of shellac to protect the surface. Artist's oil paints, in ultramarine, cobalt and a cerulean blue are mixed separately with scumble glaze, and brushed on in approximately the same quantities around the frame.

2 A stippling brush can be used to spread the colour evenly. Rags or thin plastic bags are then pressed into the paint to provide a background pattern similar to crystalline stone.

4 Dropping or spraying white spirit or turpentine onto the paint surface makes the colours "float", and this floating film of paint can form interesting and intricate patterns as the solvent reveals patches of the black base colour.

5 Marks made with a feather are much more delicate than any brushstroke. Goose feathers are the best for this purpose, as they are more robust than other types, and can be cleaned and re-used.

Sweeping strokes and a stippling motion can be tried with the feather. If necessary more paint can be applied using the feather as a brush.

7 When you have achieved the blue-on-black patterns, sprinkle on some bronze powders in small quantities. Lapis lazuli has a characteristic gold fleck. The bronze powders will adhere to the wet oil paint.

6 Make sure that there is little or no build-up of paint texture on the surface. Lapis lazuli and other semi-precious stones usually have highly polished surfaces which must be duplicated in the paint finish.

8 When the oil paint is fully dry (this could take several days), rub the surface with various grades of wet-and-dry paper until a silky, smooth surface is obtained. This can then be varnished or waxed.

VERDIGRIS

This is the attractive blue-green patina that forms on copper, brass and bronze; you see it most often on bronze-cast statuary.

It is a crystalline substance (hydrated copper acetate), which was used as a colour pigment in antiquity but proved unreliable. As a pigment it is now obsolete, but you can create a similar colour effect by using viridian (a dark bluish green) as a background colour. This can be bought in pigment form and mixed with glue (PVA or casein) or bought ready made as an emulsion paint. You will need three further colours, which can be mixed in a similar way: a pale blue, a pale green and a small quantity of yellow ochre.

When the viridian undercoat is dry, stipple on some of the paler colours in a random manner around the frame, and then throw on plenty of water to expose some of the undercoat. Finally dust some whiting or plaster over the surface so that it sticks to the paint. When dry the surplus dust can be wiped off, and matt varnish applied to protect the surface.

2 With the light colours still wet, water is dropped onto the surface to reveal parts of the viridian undercoat, which will feature in the overall finish.

1 A dark green (viridian) emulsion paint was applied as a base coat, rubbed smooth and protected with a layer of acrylic varnish. A light blue and a light green were then mixed with emulsion paint and stippled over the undercoat.

3 To create a textured, crumbly surface imitating that of real verdigris, whiting is sprinkled onto the wet paint.

4 The whiting is then dabbed with a rag to mix the powder into the paint. Be careful not to use too much whiting or the paint film will become weak and there will be a danger of it flaking off.

6 Finally, to imitate the intense green of verdigris, an oil glaze of viridian was painted all over the water paints, and a layer of matt acrylic varnish was applied.

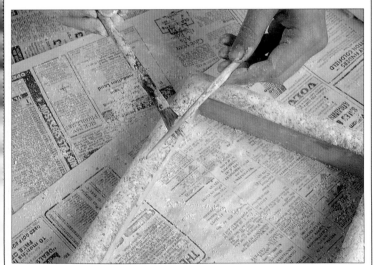

5 A water-based yellow ochre paint is spattered onto the surface by dragging a loaded brush across a stick to release small drops of colour onto the painted surface.

► This frame made by Isabella Kocum has a verdigris finish over ornament made in thick gesso (pastiglia).

SPATTERING

Spattering is an elementary exercise in decoration, but unless you work methodically you can get into a terrible mess. Take care to cover all areas around the frame, and also your eyes and face.

You can use various paints and methods depending on the effect you want. Spattering methods include knocking a paintbrush against a block of wood, thus releasing small drops of paint, stroking a paint-loaded brush against a stick, and using a toothbrush instead of a paintbrush, and drawing your thumb across it to flick the colour at the frame.

Whichever method you use, you can create different types of pattern by varying the consistency of the paint and the distance between the spattering implement and the frame. You can also spatter solvents onto a coloured paint film, which can yield a range of interesting effects.

*FURTHER INFORMATION

Paints, mediums
and varnishes   page 86

Paint and solvent
1 The frame was given a black undercoat of casein paint, providing a background to contrast with the bright top colours. A thin mixture of shellac colours is now tapped onto the surface.

2 After spattering the surface with a selection of bright colours, methylated spirits is dropped onto the paint. This separates the colour and causes it to float, so that it can be more easily manipulated.

3 When the shellac and paint have dried, it is rubbed with grade 0000 wire wool to smooth the surface.

4 Finally the surface is protected with an acrylic varnish. Be careful with the choice of varnish; some could act as a solvent on the spattered paint. Acrylic varnish is a safe choice.

RAG ROLLING AND SPONGING

Rag rolling is a method of decoration often used on large areas such as walls, but it is equally effective on frames.

The best results are obtained by mixing oil paints with the transparent oil scumble glaze* mentioned earlier. This thins the paint and allows greater flexibility. The colour is then stippled onto the frame and while still wet a rolled rag – preferably one with some texture – is pushed in varying directions along it. The rag should be moistened with white spirit or turpentine so that it can move freely without sticking.

Rag rolling is also used to soften other painted effects such as marbling and can be used for the background texture as well.

A related method is sponging, in which the texture is provided by that of the sponge. You could try out different types of sponge, both synthetic and natural.

In this case water-based colours can be used, mixed with wallpaper size, which stays wet for an hour or more to allow the sponge to be manipulated to create delicate patterns. This method can be used on paper or card as well, and is sometimes used for decorative mounts.

Sponging

1 Black water-based casein paint is sponged onto a dry red undercoat. The gilded finish on either side of the painted margin is protected with a piece of cardboard. The natural sponge leaves an interesting texture, and while the paint is still wet, it can be dampened in clean water and pressed around the frame again to thin the top colour.

▲ The rich appearance of the sponged black on red border is further amplified by the gilded sight edge and margin. The frame has been completed with a black lacquered outside edge.

► A pale green background was painted on with emulsion paint. This was allowed to dry, and then white emulsion was sponged on top with a small natural sponge.

► This frame has an ochre emulsion undercoat and a sponged finish in orange and pink water-based paints.

Rag rolling

1 A stippling brush, a stiff, round bristle-headed brush, is useful for many kinds of paint finish, as it helps to distribute the colour evenly. Here a round brush is stiffened by wrapping the head with masking tape.

3 The panel of composite board used in this example has been painted with a pale grey oil-based undercoat and then smoothed with fine sandpaper. The paint and glaze mixture is then painted onto the grey undercoat so that the whole surface is covered.

2 The oil colours are mixed with scumble glaze on a piece of glass (you can also use a palette). An artist's palette knife is used to achieve a thorough mix.

4 The stippling brush is now used to distribute the colour in an even film all over the surface. It also provides an interesting background texture.

5 A rag dampened with white spirit is then slowly rolled in various directions. This process must be done while the scumble and paint are still wet and can be manipulated easily. When dry the rolled finish can be smoothed and varnished or waxed.

6 The kind of rag chosen will affect the texture, for example a rough one such as a face flannel will leave more varied tracks and patterns. You can also experiment with different colours, perhaps using a contrasting undercoat and top coat.

▶ Here a medium-grey emulsion background is contrasted with a rag-rolled light pink oil colour.

▶ An ochre underpaint with a rag-rolled raw sienna oil colour gives a wood-like appearance to this frame.

DECOUPAGE

Decoupage, which means decorating a surface with cut pieces of coloured paper, is a method which dates back to the 18th century, or possibly even earlier, when paper began to be manufactured in large quantities. Boxes, ornaments, trays, folders, frames and even walls have been treated in this way, and the effects you can obtain are widely varied.

Any kind of paper can be used, but if you require a smooth, even surface, it should not be too thick or heavily textured. The recent developments in photocopying techniques have greatly increased the possibilities of decoupage. Now it is possible to enlarge an image, print in colour and adjust the tone to suit the subject being framed.

Pattern books of period designs, now appearing in large numbers, are an excellent source for decoupage; they can be photocopied or used directly from the books. You can also use magazine pages, wallpapers or marbled papers, either made yourself or obtained from specialist suppliers.

1 A colour photograph of a Roman wallpainting formed a suitable decorative motif for the frame. The moulding has been measured, and strips are cut to fit.

2 The corners are mitred with a scalpel for a neat appearance. Care must be taken with corners, as an overlap of paper will cause unsightly bumps, particularly if the paper is quite thick.

3 Before glueing, the decoupage paper is held against the moulding to check the fit. If any trimming needs to be done it is easier to do it before the paper is glued down.

4 The back of the paper strip is coated with white paper-glue. Wallpaper glue can also be used, but it takes longer to dry and can cause bubbling.

5 The first paper strip is carefully laid along the moulding. The glue does not dry immediately, so small adjustments can be made as you work.

6 The second strip is now put into place, with care taken to ensure that the corners meet properly. When all the paper has been applied, the frame should be given several coats of varnish, either matt or gloss depending on the effect you want.

▶ In this frame by Isabella Kocum black and white photocopies taken from some 18th century engravings were glued on with dilute PVA glue and the frame was then varnished.

▼ This mirror frame, made by Jacqueline Beard, is decorated with cut-out jam-pot labels. The background was cracked using "crackleur" varnishes, and brown oil paint was rubbed into the cracks (see Crackle finishes page 92). The frame was then given several layers of varnish to protect the finish and blend the decoupage decorations into the overall surface.

CHAPTER 7

GILDING

Traditionally, gilding is done with gold leaf, but gold colours are also made from a mixture of other metals, mainly brass and copper. These imitation golds are obtainable either as fine powders, thin metal leaf, or manufactured into gold paint and gold wax. They are more often used than genuine gold leaf because they are much cheaper and easier to apply, and if the surface of the frame is well prepared, there is no reason why these base-metal "golds" should not make attractive finishes.

However, all forms of gold colour will sooner or later tarnish and become much duller. This may take five to ten years, but the gold colour will progressively darken through oxidation. Pure gold, on the other hand, whether solid gold or gold leaf, will not tarnish, and has thus been treasured through the ages. A gilded frame may become dusty and dirty with age, but careful cleaning of the gold can restore its brightness (unless the gold has been varnished or lacquered, in which case it is not so easy).

The purity of gold is expressed in "carat", with pure gold being described as 24 carat. Most gilders use 22 carat or $23\frac{1}{2}$ carat, although there are plenty of grades of alloy leaf at 18, 12 and 9 carat. Gold is often mixed with other metals to change the colour and to extend the content. For example, white gold is made with silver to produce a warm silver colour, while copper is added to gold to make the colour more red. There is also lemon gold and green gold.

The purer the gold leaf is, the softer and more malleable it is to use. But, of course, it is also more expensive. Silver, being a heavier and less expensive leaf, is recommended for practice by beginners.

Apart from the purity and colour, gold is also differentiated into weight. Suppliers talk of single or double gold. This is slightly confusing, because the double is not usually double the thickness, but just heavier. This heavier gold has more covering potential than the single thickness, and when burnished does not show the undercolour of clay.

PREPARING THE SURFACE

Whether you are using real gold leaf or one of the many imitations, it is necessary to have a smooth even surface to work on. All metal finishes are reflective, and will show up any flaws in the surface of the frame very clearly. The most painstaking care is required for the water gilding* method, because the gold is burnished afterwards to increase its lustre, and this polishing with a burnishing tool requires a smooth and slightly soft surface. The other gold finishes do not need such a demanding surface and can be painted with undercoat or acrylic gesso and then rubbed down with fine sandpaper.

On all but the most seasoned woods the corners of the frame are susceptible to movement, which means that in time cracks will appear along the mitre. To prevent this, thin strips of fine material should be glued over the joins before the frame is coated with gesso. This is used to fill the grain of the wood and to give a smooth surface for the gold.

Applying gesso
To seal the wood and make it less absorbent, first put on two coats of size, allowing drying time between coats. Using a brush, apply eight to ten coats of gesso, always working in the same direction. Allow it to dry slightly but not completely between coats; gesso is stronger if each coat is applied when the last is still slightly damp, so that they combine to form one strong skin.

If air bubbles appear use a damp finger to rub the gesso lightly between coats.

When the gesso has dried thoroughly, use wet-and-dry paper to sand it smooth. The initial rubbing down can be done with coarse (180 grade) wet-and-dry paper used with plenty of water. Rub up and down along one side of the frame, and when you can feel the surface is even, wipe off the excess water with cotton wool. Repeat this procedure on the remaining sides of the frame. The surface is now ready to be rubbed down with finer papers, starting with 400 grade and finishing with 500 or 600.

＊FURTHER INFORMATION

Water gilding   page 114

Gesso
1 All wood moves with changes of atmosphere, and gesso is brittle when dry, so that there is a danger of it cracking along the mitre joint. Here the joint has been protected by glueing a strip of silk over it.

2 For a smooth surface, gesso should be put on with a soft brush such as an artist's sable. There are various ways of creating textures if desired (see opposite page), but the gesso must be made thicker.

3 When the gesso is dry it must be rubbed down with wet-and-dry paper, used with water. It is possible to use dry sandpaper, but it will make a great deal of dust. Rub one side of the frame, continuing until you can feel that the gesso is smooth, then wipe off the excess water with cotton wool and repeat the procedure for the other sides.

Engraving
1 Before applying burnishing clay and gold leaf, the gesso can be textured or engraved with a pattern, which makes an interesting contrast to plain areas of burnished leaf. Here a pattern is traced onto a smooth gesso base. Carbon paper can also be used below the tracing paper.

2 To make the engraved lines, wet the drawing slightly to soften the gesso, and then score into it with a sharp point. You can use a special engraving tool or improvise one by pushing a nail into a piece of cork. For deep-relief engraving, eight or more coats of gesso need to be applied.

TEXTURES UNDER GOLD

Texture underneath gold or silver will form bright highlights that break up the surface and increase the reflected light. In this sample grains of couscous, sandpaper and a piece of crochet work have been glued onto a panel, painted with gesso and burnishing clay and gilded. Between the sandpaper and the crochet material there is a strip of stippled gesso which has been left as a rough surface.

RECIPE FOR GESSO

Ingredients
● Whiting (calcium carbonate, commonly known as chalk). The best is "gilder's whiting", which has been sieved into a fine powder. If coarser whiting is used it must be sieved and ground in a pestle and mortar.
● Rabbit-skin size (glue). This is sold in sheet, granule or fine dust form. The sheets have to be soaked in water overnight, but granules and dust can be mixed to make size immediately.

Place in a pan containing warm water and heat gently until the granules or powder have dissolved. It is important not to overheat, as this will destroy the adhesion of the size.

To make the size
Make a mixture of eight parts water and one part glue. Put into a container (such as an empty tin or jamjar).

To make the gesso
Take the required quantity of warmed size and sprinkle in whiting until it settles just below the surface. Stir the mixture slowly and carefully with a brush, taking care not to stir in air bubbles.

BURNISHING CLAY

Burnishing clay, or "bole", as it is sometimes called, is used as a preparatory stage to the traditional method of water gilding*. It is applied over the gessoed and sanded surface, and forms a soft bed for the gold leaf. The action of water on the clay also allows the gold leaf to adhere.

It is not necessary to use burnishing clay as an undercoat for transfer gilding* or imitation gold finishes*, but it is widely used for these methods, partly because of its attractive colours and partly because the smooth, matt surface of the clay provides a good foundation for these finishes.

The clay is bought either in liquid form or as a solid cone. The liquid is easier both to obtain and to use; the cones have to be finely ground in a pestle and mortar. The traditional colour used under gold leaf is a terracotta or red and either black or blue for silver. Ochre or yellow is often used over ornamental surfaces so that tiny faults in the gold surface do not show. A range of other colours is available from specialist suppliers.

Preparation and application
For the first coat, re-heat the size solution used in the preparation of gesso* and then dilute it with one part of water to two parts of size solution. Dissolve enough clay into it to give a good colour. Apply one coat, and leave to dry completely.

For the following coats, dilute the size made for gesso with two parts of water to three parts size, and dissolve the clay into it to make the consistency of single cream. Apply four coats, allowing each to dry thoroughly, and keeping the clay warm throughout. When the last coat has dried, rub down carefully with wet-and-dry paper or fine (grade 0000) steel wool to obtain a smooth, silky and evenly coloured surface.

*FURTHER INFORMATION

Water gilding	page 114
Transfer gilding	page 118
Imitation gold finishes	page 127

Gilding and painting
1 The whole frame has been gessoed and rubbed to a smooth finish. In this example, the central margin of the frame will be used for a decorative paint finish with two gold strips on either side, so the burnishing clay is applied only to those areas.

2 Four coats of clay are necessary as a foundation for gilding. Full drying time must be allowed between each coat, and the clay must be kept warm throughout. When the last coat has dried, rub down the clay with 0000 steel wool. If there are any lumps or texture they may have to be removed with fine sandpaper.

3 The central margin is painted with a crimson acrylic as an undercoat for the decorative paint finish. Gilding can be done before or after the paint finish. Both methods are used and both have advantages and disadvantages.

2 A first coat of burnishing clay is applied with a sable brush. This will dry more quickly than subsequent coats (in about ten to twenty minutes) as it is absorbed into the gesso. The clay changes colour as it dries so you will know when to paint the next coat.

Preparing for gilding
1 The gesso on top of the composition figures has been rubbed smooth in preparation for the burnishing clay. This is a difficult task over an ornamented surface, so careful painting of the gesso is essential to avoid a tedious rubbing-down process.

3 The subsequent coats are made creamier with more clay and slightly less glue. Keep the clay warm as you paint each layer, and do not overload your brush. The final coat is left to dry and then rubbed to a smooth silky finish, using 0000 steel wool and 600 grade sandpaper.

WATER GILDING

Water gilding is the traditional method of gilding, in which the gold or silver leaf is laid onto a surface prepared with gesso and burnishing clay and then burnished with a special tool to give a brilliant lustre. The only adhesive used is "gilder's water", which is simply water with a minute amount of glue added. The action of the water on the clay causes the very thin leaves to stick, and the lack of glue allows an even-pressured polish with the burnisher.

The process requires both patience and skill, but is the most highly prized of the gilt finishes. In addition to the gold or silver leaves you will need a gilder's pad, knife and tip, as shown in the photograph.

Mixing the gilder's water correctly is crucial; too much glue can result in unattractive brown marks on the leaf. Put a pea-sized piece of the glue mixed for gesso* into half a pint of water, heat gently until dissolved, and when cool add three tablespoons of ethyl alcohol or methylated spirits.

Deposit some leaves of gold at the back of the pad, holding the book open with both hands so that the gold falls easily, then lift a leaf with the knife, place it at the front and breathe gently on it to flatten it before cutting to the required dimension with a firm, even pressure.

Vigorously brush your hair or cheek with the gilder's tip, which should deposit enough oil on it to allow you to pick up the gold, then pick it up with about a centimetre showing at the top of the tip and leave it there while you brush over the clay with plenty of gilder's water. If you find the leaf does not adhere to the tip, rub a little vaseline on your wrist and lightly brush the tip over it, but use it very sparingly, as too much vaseline will prevent the leaf from being released cleanly onto the frame.

Place the gold carefully into position. It will be released from the brush as soon as it makes contact with the clay. Repeat the procedure again, allowing the leaves to overlap slightly, and after you have finished a "run" along one side, gently press the leaves with a ball of cotton wool.

Leave the leaf for at least two hours before burnishing. To do this, press the agate lightly over the leaf, slightly increasing the pressure, and testing the surface as you work. To achieve a uniform lustre it is best to burnish the whole frame lightly and then go over it again with greater pressure.

✻FURTHER INFORMATION

Recipe for gesso   page 111

Gilding equipment
It is possible to improvise a gilding kit using some suede or fine leather stuck onto a board and a kitchen knife with an even but not too sharp an edge. However, for anyone contemplating a large amount of gilding it is better and more convenient to buy a professional set of tools like the ones shown here. A gilder's cushion with a draught barrier attached so that loose gold can be kept at the back. A gilder's knife, which has an even but slightly dull blade. It cuts the gold cleanly without damaging the cushion. A gilder's tip for picking up the gold leaf. These come in a variety of sizes and qualities. A gilder's mop brush for pressing the gold into awkward areas. A burnishing stick, which is made of agate set in a wooden handle. A book of loose-leaf gold, these usually have 25 leaves approximately 8 cm (3⅛ in) square.

Gilding a panel
1 Gilder's water is brushed onto the surface of the clay to help the gold leaf adhere to it. Be generous with the gilder's water.

2 It is best to pick up the gold from the pad with the gilder's tip before applying the water. The gold will stick to the tip until it is released onto the frame. If you paint the water on first and then pick up the gold there is a danger that the water will have dried too much.

4 To pick up the gold, brush the gilder's tip across your hair or face, which picks up just enough oil for the gold to stick. Then place the tip firmly onto the leaf, leaving a small border visible, and lift the brush from the pad.

3 Until you are practised at gilding and can pick up whole squares of gold with confidence it is easier to cut up the leaves of gold into small pieces. These are less tricky to lift and put into place. Here the gilder's knife is pushed firmly back and forth, cutting the gold cleanly.

5 The leaf will be released from the brush as soon as it touches the dampened clay. After a few minutes it can be pressed flat using a piece of cotton wool, and further pieces laid, allowing each to overlap slightly.

6 The agate tools used for burnishing are made in various shapes and sizes to suit different moulding profiles. The broad, flat area is used – do not dig in with the tip. Rub gently at first to test the softness of the gesso, and then gradually build up the pressure until a bright, overall lustre is achieved.

▲ This cassetta-style frame made by Patrick Ireland has a water-gilded sight edge and an ivory gesso border divided into plates. The inner glazed frame and border are surrounded by a black-lacquered "Hogarth" frame with gilt ball decoration.

7 For this frame, the final stage was to distress the gold leaf with beeswax, particularly the figures at the top. The background of the top panel was coated with acrylic varnish to make a contrasting matt surface. The frame is a tabernacle style with the top panel decorated with Neo-classical putti and fluted pillars on the sides. The top and bottom are faced with coving.

Gilding ornament

1 Applying leaf over decoration is trickier than laying it on a flat surface, as there can be a problem with covering all the recesses. If these are painted with a light yellow ochre clay, a similar tone and colour to the gold, it will be less noticeable if the gold does not quite reach the bottom of the recess.

3 In awkward areas of the corner decoration a gilder's mop is used to press the gold into place. This is an invaluable tool, which can also be used to clean off excess pieces of gold.

2 In this example the relief decoration on the corners is quite deep. Black burnishing clay was painted all over the frame before the corner recesses were coated in yellow. The leaf is then laid in the same way as in the previous demonstration.

4 The gold continues to be laid all round the frame, starting with the top edge. After burnishing it will be distressed to reveal some of the black clay colour underneath. The areas normally chosen for distressing are the highest parts, such as the "peaks" of the decoration, thus artificially simulating a process which would occur naturally with time.

TRANSFER GILDING

The main difference between transfer gilding and water gilding is that glue is used in the latter process instead of gilder's water, which makes it impossible to burnish the leaf. The lustre is thus less bright, but transfer gilding has many advantages. It is considerably faster (and is thus the process used for most commercially made pre-decorated mouldings), it is more robust, and because it is not burnished the gesso surface does not need such elaborate preparation.

The leaf sold for transfer gilding is backed with paper, hence the name of the process, but you can also use loose leaf. The traditional glue is a viscous substance called oil gold size, but in recent times a water-soluble glue has been developed, which is easier to use and more flexible in terms of drying time (gold size dries quickly).

However, gold size is stronger, so is better for any gilding that may be subject to stress. It must be painted evenly onto the surface to be gilded, as otherwise the thinner areas of glue will be ready for gilding before the rest. It should be just a little tacky, so test it by placing your knuckle or the back of your hand against it. If it pulls too obviously, wait a little longer before laying the leaf.

Water-based glue will be ready for the leaf in fifteen minutes after application, and since it stays usable for much longer, you do not need to rush with the gilding.

Both types of glue are suitable for transfer leaf, loose leaf and the heavier imitation metal leafs*.

*FURTHER INFORMATION

Imitation gold
    finishes   page 127

Using gold leaf

1 It is not necessary to use gesso on a frame that is to be transfer gilded, but it should be painted with some form of undercoat. Here a thick undercoat of black casein paint was used (black burnishing clay is frequently used underneath water-gilded silver). A water-based gold size, a modern alternative to the oil gold size used in the past, was painted evenly on top of the black paint.

2 After about fifteen minutes the water size is dry enough to start laying the leaf. Transfer leaf is the same as loose leaf except it has been pressed onto transparent paper, which makes it easier to apply.

Using imitation gold

1 This frame is a traditional Hogarth type, which usually has a black central margin and a gilded outer edge and sight edge. The sight edge has been painted with terracotta clay to resemble the traditional gilded finish. Water gold size is now applied on top preparatory to gilding.

2 The imitation gold leaf (sometimes called "Dutch" or "schlagg" leaf) used in this example is loose rather than paper-backed leaf. It can be cut up into the appropriate sizes with a craft knife.

4 To press the leaf firmly over the underlying ornament, tissue or thin plastic can be used as a barrier so that no glue is transferred to the fingers. This makes it easier to stick the gold closely to the surface of the frame. Imitation gold and silver leaf, and silver alloy leaves need to be protected from tarnishing by applying coats of shellac or other specialist lacquers.

3 Unlike genuine gold or silver leaf, this can be picked up with the fingers and placed into position, or thin card can be folded and used as tweezers to pick it up.

Commercial mouldings
A wide variety of ready made gilded mouldings finishes is available from framing suppliers.

PASTIGLIA

This is a thick gesso* suitable for ornamental work on frames. The ratio of glue to water is the same as the recipe given on the previous pages, the difference being that more whiting is used. For the ordinary gesso, the glue was filled almost to the surface with whiting, but in this case whiting is added until a thick, creamy mixture is obtained.

There are many fine examples of pastiglia work on period Italian frames. This technique can also be used for creating a more contemporary ornamental surface. Pastiglia is usually applied on top of a previously gessoed and sanded surface, and is then gilded.

The characteristic appearance of pastiglia is one in which the ornament appears almost to have grown out of the gesso. It is an ideal technique for achieving fine pattern work.

＊FURTHER INFORMATION

Recipe for gesso   page 111

1 A pattern was chosen from a book of designs and then traced out. A simple, bold pattern is most suitable for pastiglia decoration; too many intricate details are difficult to execute.

2 The traced design is now transferred to the frame. It is usual to apply pastiglia decoration to a surface already prepared with gesso, as this makes it easier to smooth the pattern. This frame has had eight coats of gesso, rubbed smooth.

3 The thick pastiglia mixture is painted onto the drawn design. Do not apply too much at once; but build up the three-dimensional shapes gradually. The pastiglia gesso is so thick, however, that three or four coats will produce a substantial depth. It should not be allowed to dry in between coats; you can apply another one as soon as the glossy wet shine has disappeared.

4 When the design is complete, but before the pastiglia is fully dry, rub it with a damp and slightly textured cloth. This smooths it out, and is much easier than rubbing down an ornamented surface when it is hard and dry.

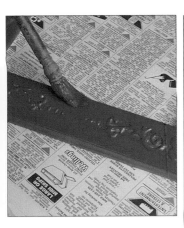

5 When the pastiglia is quite dry it may be necessary to do some final finishing with dry sandpaper before applying the burnishing clay. Four coats of terracotta burnishing clay are painted onto the surface, allowing each to dry before the next is applied.

6 Gilder's water is brushed onto the clay, and the gold or silver leaf is laid on the wet clay. The transfer gilding method can also be used, but the bright burnished surface achieved by water gilding and burnishing shows pastiglia ornament to the best advantage.

7 The gold has been cut into appropriate sized pieces, and is picked up and lifted onto the frame with a gilder's tip.

8 The brilliant lustre achieved by burnishing displays the pastiglia ornament to advantage. It can sometimes overwhelm a picture, however, and various methods can be used after burnishing for culling or distressing it.

▶ This frame, inspired by Art Nouveau decorations and the paintings of Gustav Klimt, incorporates flat painted borders with textured pastiglia decoration and gilded sections.

▶ This inventive design was made in thick pastiglia. The lizards, in high relief, have been burnished, and the background was later punched and distressed to create textural contrast. Both frames were made by Isabella Kocum.

FINISHES OVER GILDING

Burnished gold leaf is very bright and lustrous, an effect which is not suitable for all pictures – it can be overpowering. Gilders have devised a variety of different techniques for reducing the brilliance of the gold and subtly toning the surface.

Distressing gold and silver

This involves rubbing off some of the leaf to expose the clay beneath, which gives a pleasing mature colour to the gold or silver. It is much easier to distress water-gilded* leaf than transfer leaf* because there is very little glue used in the water-gilding process. The amount you distress the leaf is a matter of personal taste. On some frames it is so distressed that only the double-thickness overlap across both leaves is left. More often, however, the leaf is lightly rubbed to hint at the colour below.

Matt and colour effects

The simplest method of producing a matt finish while preserving the colour of the leaf is to leave certain areas unburnished. You can see this effect on the frame illustrated on page 108, where only the ornamental motifs have been burnished. The unburnished areas are more vulnerable to

damage, and so a thin coat of shellac* is often used on top. You can also dull the surface of burnished gold by painting shellac, matt acrylic varnish or a thin solution of rabbit-skin size* over it.

Tortoiseshell effect

The traditional method was to lay real tortoiseshell over a silver ground, which was often tinted red to give a richer colour below the shell. The same applies to the fake plastic tortoiseshell used here; a silver ground gives a more brilliant translucence. Another type of tortoiseshell effect is made with earth colours suspended in shellac varnish, dropped onto a silver surface.

Sgraffito

This is another traditional technique, in which egg tempera colour is laid over a gilded finish and then scratched into, revealing the gold beneath. Tempera is ideal because it does not adhere strongly to the gold, but other water-based colours such as acrylic and casein can also be used for this technique.

*FURTHER INFORMATION

Water gilding	page 114
Transfer gilding	page 118
Rabbit-skin size, see	
recipe for gesso	page 111
Paints, mediums	
and varnishes	page 86

▲ **Distressed gold**
The effects you can obtain by distressing gold and silver leaf are extremely varied. Here the gold has been distressed to a matt surface which marries well with the bands of paintwork in the recesses of the moulding. The small specks of burnishing clay showing through the gold give an attractive slightly textured effect.

Painted tortoiseshell
1 A group of earth pigments have been mixed with shellac and painted onto a silvered frame. For this process it is best to limit the colour range, and here only three are used, yellow ochre, burnt sienna and raw umber. As with the other painted imitation finishes, it is useful to have some reference material to hand, either photographs or the real thing. Unless attention is paid to the distinctive markings, this finish can bear more resemblance to leopard skin.

2 The colours need to be kept wet so that they can be manipulated with thin plastic bags, feathers or rags, as in the marble and lapis lazuli finishes shown in the previous chapter. This is done by spraying methylated spirits on top. When the background textured pattern is formed you can start to paint in the distinctive dark markings, which are usually rounded at the edges and merge into one another.

3 When sufficient marks have been made the shellac must be allowed to dry thoroughly; this will take twenty-four hours. The finish is then rubbed smooth using fine grades of wet-and-dry paper and steel wool. Some top coats of shellac can be applied to give a smooth finish, and can be tinted with colour to harmonize with the overall effect. For a silk finish, rub some steel wool with wax over the frame and polish with a duster.

This oval frame, made by Robert Cunning, has an undercolour of imitation metal leaf, which reflects light through the paint finish. The tortoiseshell markings were made with oil colour and scumble glaze, and warm earth colours were stippled and feathered on to the gold ground. When the paint was dry the frame was rubbed smooth and then waxed.

Artificial tortoiseshell

1 The frame was first painted with a black undercoat and then transfer gilded with silver leaf. A red shellac varnish is painted onto the silver prior to sticking down the plastic tortoiseshell. The silver ground will reflect light through the tortoiseshell, which would otherwise be dull and lacklustre. The red shellac seals the silver and prevents tarnishing, but also has a decorative function, giving a richer light to the tortoiseshell. The method shown here is the traditional one used in the past for real tortoiseshell on frames.

3 Thin strips have been cut to fit the central margin of the frame, and the corners are now trimmed to a 45° angle to form a mitre join. Tortoiseshell frames were popular in 17th-century Holland. The shell often came in short plates that were attached to the flat borders of ebony frames.

4 A strong glue is needed to stick the plastic onto the frame, and here contact adhesive is used. On period frames the plates were held by small pieces of ebony beading.

2 Tortoiseshell is now a prohibited import, so the plastic imitation must be used instead. It resembles the genuine article in texture, depth and colour, and can be very effective. It is easy to cut with a sharp craft knife.

5 The contact adhesive is applied to both surfaces, left for a few minutes to allow the glue to harden a little, and the two surfaces brought together. The plastic tortoiseshell has the advantage of needing no other protection or finish, and its semi-matt surface closely resembles real tortoiseshell.

Sgraffito
1 The frame was water gilded and burnished before covering with four coats of ultramarine egg tempera and left to dry. The design was transferred onto the paint by tracing with a soft pencil and the engraving was made by working over the traced design with a sharpened piece of wood.

2 When the sgraffito design was complete, circles of decorative star were punched in the corners (the punching method is shown overleaf).

▲ In this frame made by Isabella Kocum, silver leaf was burnished and then distressed to reveal red burnishing clay. Blue acrylic paint was then laid on top and scratched away to make the silver and red pattern.

► This copy of an 18th-century Italian frame made by Robert Cunning has sgraffito acanthus leaf decoration in the corners and centre.

► A classical running wave pattern has been scratched through black tempera paint to reveal the water-gilded surface underneath. The frame was made by Isabella Kocum.

PUNCHED AND ENGRAVED DESIGNS

Breaking up the surface of the gold or silver, either by making punch marks after gilding or by engraving into the gesso before gilding can give more light and variety of texture to the frame.

An ordinary nail punch will leave a circular pattern in the gold which when repeated as an overall design can be very attractive. More elaborate punch motifs can be purchased from specialist shops.

Gesso is a soft surface and can be very easily textured by making scratched designs; the thicker it is the deeper your scratch marks can be. Other methods include stippling with a thick gesso mix and sticking textured fabric onto the wood before applying the gesso.

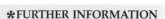

✱FURTHER INFORMATION

Recipe for gesso   page 111

The engraved pattern on this frame by Isabella Kocum was made in the gesso before gilding. The delicate design is reinforced by the contrast of textures; only the areas inside the engraved lines have been burnished.

▼ **Punched designs**
Punching is usually done after gilding. This frame has been gilded in silver leaf over a pastiglia design, and a close pattern of punch marks provides a contrast to the burnished highlights. The leaf is not broken by the punch, but pressed into the soft gesso beneath, so you can hit it quite hard.

IMITATION GOLD FINISHES

Those who do not want to spend a great deal of time and money on a perfect gold finish may find one of the various imitation golds a useful alternative. Manufacturers now produce very convincing imitation gold and silver leafs, which when used well can be almost indistinguishable from the real thing. Unfortunately they do tarnish with time, and need to be protected with a varnish or lacquer, which robs the finish of the subtlety and glow of real gold or silver. They are applied using glue, as described in the section on transfer gilding.

Gold paints can be obtained ready made, or you can mix them yourself using bronze powders and a medium such as shellac, PVA or rabbit-skin glue. These powders are usually made from bronze and thus called bronze powders, but have the appearance of gold or silver, and are made in a variety of colours and qualities. The best, called burnishing powders, are finely ground, and when suspended in shellac make a quick-drying and effective paint.

Gold and silver waxes can produce an effect very similar to real metal leaf if applied over a surface prepared with gesso and burnishing clay.

Applying the gold
1 For the best results, gold wax should be applied with a soft rag over a surface prepared with gesso and burnishing clay.

2 It can then be burnished with an agate tool in the usual way. The gold used here is that made to the recipe shown on the right. It is thicker and more lustrous than most ready made gold waxes.

RECIPE FOR GOLD OR SILVER WAX

Materials
● Carnauba wax
● Beeswax
● Turpentine or white spirit
● Bronze powder

Method
Place beeswax and carnauba wax (in a proportion of approximately four of beeswax to one of carnauba) in a tin.

Cover with turpentine or white spirit and heat gently in a saucepan of water.

When the waxes have melted, test the mixture by pouring a little onto a non-absorbent surface such as glass or plastic. It should solidify in about ten seconds. If it sets almost immediately, it is too hard, so add more white spirit. If it takes too long to set, add more wax. When the mixture is right, use a knife to mix in as much powder as you can, until it becomes crumbly. Store in an airtight jar or tin. The wax is usually applied with a rag or a finger, but can be thinned with white spirit to make a paint.

CHAPTER 8

RESTORATION AND REPAIR

Old frames are often poorly preserved, with their gilding, paint or other decorative finishes cracked, chipped and weathered. Most old wood frames can be cleaned and restored quite easily, though frames with decoration on a gesso surface may present more of a problem, particularly if they have been kept in a damp place. Damp tends to crack and soften gesso, and this can make restoration impossible.

A lot of the frames bought from auctions and antique shops are of the 19th and early 20th centuries. They are usually made of ornamental composition in gold or silver, or plain wood with a paint or gilt finish over a gesso ground. Even the most humble frames in the 19th century were gilded, often in silver with a yellow wash to emulate gold.

Although such frames may not be particularly valuable they are worth preserving and restoring as long as they are not too badly damaged. Some frames, unfortunately, are so far gone in decay that it is not worth the time and expense. If the gesso is flaking off in large lumps this usually means that the adhesion between the wood and the gesso has deteriorated to the point that it is no longer worth renovating. In such a case, the frame itself may still be usable, and if it's an attractive shape it's worth soaking off the gesso and composition. This is easily done by wrapping wet rags around the frame and leaving overnight to soften. In the morning the gesso and composition will scrape off easily.

For valuable, carved and moulded frames it is best to seek expert advice before attempting restoration, as a poor repair can reduce the value of the frame. A useful standard to apply, is that any restoration should be invisible, and if possible repaired with the same materials as the original frame.

CLEANING FRAMES

Old frames usually need to be cleaned, but unless great care is taken there is a risk of destroying the patina of age, which can be an attractive feature, or of removing areas of gilding. For wood and painted frames a light cleaning mixture of ammonia and water (one part ammonia to eight parts water) is all that is generally required. When dry the frame can be polished with wax. If you want to remove varnish from the surface you will have to use the appropriate solvent. There are several brands of general-purpose varnish remover, which can be thinned with water or oil depending on the type of remover. This will give you more control during the cleaning process.

When cleaning an old gilt frame even more care is needed. The leaf is so thin that a heavy hand or a strong solution of cleaner can remove the gilt completely in a matter of seconds. It is safer to start with a weak solution of cleaner, which unless there is a top layer of lacquer or varnish, is usually ammonia and water. Try a mix of sixteen parts water to one of ammonia, and if this is not effective, add more ammonia. Apply the cleaner lightly with a brush and then gently dab off the moisture with cotton wool. Be careful not to wipe with the cotton wool, as this too can lift the gold leaf.

For gold or silver which has been lacquered or varnished try using acetone or methylated spirits in a similarly careful way. If this does not work then try one of the proprietary brands of varnish remover, suitably diluted.

Antique patina
When you have cleaned the surface and repaired* any damage, there remains the problem of matching the antique patina. Sometimes a little colour pigment added to wax and then rubbed onto the cleaned part is sufficient, but for larger areas it may be easier to use colour in the form of paint.

2 While the frame is still wet, lightly dab with cotton wool to lift the dirt. Do not rub with the cotton wool, as this may remove the gold as well.

1 Apply the diluted ammonia with a paintbrush, working over a small area at a time, and pushing the brush into the crevices of the moulding. If the ammonia mixture starts to remove any of the gilded surface, dilute it with more water, but if the dirt is stubborn, add more ammonia.

3 When the frame is clean, it is important to neutralize any residue of ammonia with water. Work over the frame with clean water and a brush, and then dab again with cotton wool.

This could either be a solution of rabbit-skin glue* mixed with watercolour or dry pigment, or oil paint used very thinly in the form of a glaze. The advantage of glue and watercolour is that it can be removed or modified without damaging the surface by carefully applying warm water on a brush.

A quick way to mellow the surface of gold or silver is to apply bitumen paint. This can be rubbed on with a cloth or painted with a brush, and if you want to reduce the effect you can wipe it down with a cloth dipped in white spirit. A thin film of this black-brown colour is very effective as an ageing patina and lends a subtle darkness to the gilding. On silver, you can obtain a similar effect by applying a chemical, ammonium hydrosulphide. It should be used sparingly or the silver will turn very dark, or you can thin it with water before application, to reduce this effect. The smell of sulphur is not pleasant, so keep the lid on as much as possible.

To distress either paint or transfer gilding* use fine steel wool and a cutting compound such as pumice or rottenstone. This polishes the surface and can remove a little of the top coat to reveal the colour below.

*FURTHER INFORMATION

Ammonium hydrosulphide

1 New silver looks very bright, but will tarnish to a dull brown or black if it is left unprotected. Some discolouration will occur after a few months, and this can look attractive. The frame can then be protected with lacquer to prevent further tarnishing. Here the discolouring process is artificially induced by using hydrosulphide to patinate a newly made silver-gilt frame.

2 The undiluted chemical will turn the silver a dark brown, so for lighter effects it needs to be diluted with water. It takes an hour or more for the chemical to react fully, after which it must be neutralized with water, or it will continue to darken the silver.

Bitumen

Another way to darken silver or gold is to apply bitumen paint. This heavy brown colour is painted on the gilt surface with a brush and then lightly wiped off with a cloth. It dries quickly, so work in small areas, wiping it off as you progress around the frame. When dry the bitumen can be easily removed with white spirits or turpentine.

REPAIR AND REJOINING

Many old frames are so well constructed that the mitre joints remain tight even though the glue has perished. This is usually because there is a brace of some kind across the mitre. If there are no obvious gaps in the joints it is safer to leave them alone, but if there are gaps, and the frame is still nailed together, you can often put glue into the joints without removing the nails. The large tapered nails often used on old frames are difficult to extract without damaging the corners. If the joints are badly damaged it may be necessary to pull the frame apart, trim the mitres and reassemble.

The most commonly used glue in restoration work is the animal-based carpenter's glue, known as pearl glue. This is useful because it can be softened by heat, and if any adjustment needs to be made, a kitchen knife heated over a flame and then inserted into the join will loosen the bond so that the join can be shifted.

Although still used by restorers and other craftsmen, pearl glue has largely been replaced by PVA, which requires no heat, dries quickly and is transparent when dry.

Re-glueing
1 In this frame the old glue had perished, but the nails still held the frame together although the joins were loose. Rather than damage the frame by extracting the nails fresh glue (PVA) was put into the join.

2 Mitre corner clips are useful for clamping the corners securely while the glue dries.

3 Although the clips do leave small marks on the corners, they are adaptable, and can be used to exert pressure on different areas of the frame. This is an advantage with old frames, because often the wood has warped and a lot of pressure is needed to obtain a tight join.

4 While the clip is still in place, new nails are hammered into the corner to strengthen the joint. It is safer to drill holes first, as otherwise you may split the wood when hammering. Any marks can be filled and coloured to blend into the side of the frame.

Before and after
This early 19th-century frame was extensively damaged, particularly in the corners. Moulds (see pages 134-135) were made of the existing pieces of ornament, and then one complete corner was moulded and modelled. The other three corners were then made from a mould of this corner. The frame was cleaned with ammonia and water, and all the repairs were re-gilded and then coloured to match the existing patina.

REPLACING BROKEN ORNAMENT

Although some minor repairs can be made to a chipped frame by modelling with a knife and filler, any pattern or ornament must be remade and replaced. This is done by making a mould from an undamaged area of the frame, taking an impression from this and then glueing the new piece onto the frame. Usually the ornament is in fairly shallow relief, and can be reproduced using one-piece moulds.

Making the mould

There are many different materials from which moulds can be made. In the past, carved box-wood moulds were used, later superseded by industrial gelatine and plaster. We now have, among other substances, fibre-glass, latex rubber and silicone rubber. Fibre-glass, used by professional mouldmakers, is messy and gives off noxious fumes, so is not suitable for home use. Moulds can also be made from wax, epoxy resin and plasticine. These do not give fine definition, but are adequate for simple patterns.

Silicone rubber, on the other hand, gives excellent definition and is easy to use. It comes in two parts, the silicone, which is white, and the catalyst, which is coloured. The more catalyst you use the faster the rubber hardens, but care must be taken not to add too much or it will become "buttery" before a good impression has been obtained.

To give more firmness to the mould the back is usually given a coat of plaster, but a good alternative to plaster is the kind of silicone rubber that plumbers use around the edges of baths and basins. This is sold in syringe tubes.

For quick-disposable moulds, there is a seaweed-based medium used by dentists and the food industry.

Silicone rubber

1 To protect the surface of the frame, apply a light coat of linseed oil to the place where the moulding medium is to go.

2 The red catalyst is mixed into the white silicone rubber. With this particular type the more catalyst you add the more quickly the rubber will harden.

3 The buttery silicone rubber is applied to the frame with a knife. Make sure that any small cracks and undercuts in the ornament are filled before the rubber is put into place, otherwise it will be difficult to lift the mould without damaging the frame.

This is a powder which when mixed with water forms a firm jelly. It gives a good definition and sets very fast, but unfortunately it does not last more than twenty-four hours, and is thus only suitable for small areas of ornament. As with the silicone rubber, a firm plaster back will make it easier to take an impression.

Taking the impression
Once the mould has been made, an impression is taken by filling it with some form of composition such as that given in the recipe overleaf. You can

Alginate
1 Again, linseed oil is applied to protect the surface of the frame before the alginate moulding medium is put into place.

2 The seaweed-based medium is mixed to a smooth paste with approximately its own volume of water. It is then applied with a knife. Alginate dries fast, so you must work quickly.

4 When the rubber has set, lift it gently off the frame. Larger moulds will benefit from a backing of plaster or more silicone rubber, so that the mould will not distort when an impression is taken.

3 Fresh alginate will not combine with alginate that has already set, so the medium is only suitable for small repairs. However, it has good definition. Like silicone rubber, it is flexible, and will need a rigid backing of plaster.

RECIPE FOR COMPOSITION

This is a traditional recipe, variations of which have been used on picture frames for over 200 years.

Ingredients
- Rabbit-skin glue
- Soft toilet paper
- Whiting
- Linseed oil

Method
The main base is a strong mixture of rabbit-skin glue. Mix it in a tin heated in a saucepan of water, as in the recipe for gesso, but in a proportion of three parts water to one of glue. When it has melted, remove it from the hot water and put it to one side.

Now take some toilet paper and put it into the water of the saucepan (you will need about five sheets to ½ pint of water), bring to the boil and leave in boiling water for about a minute.

Take out the resulting pulp and leave to cool, then break it up into small pieces and add to the glue. Heat this mixture until thoroughly combined.

Now put in enough whiting to make the consistency of firm bread dough, stirring with a knife until it comes off the sides of the tin in lumps.

Finally, add two or three tablespoons of linseed oil and stir again, keeping the composition warm until you begin to use it.

also use plaster for this, but because it cannot be removed from the mould until it is rigid, it can only be attached to a flat surface. The beauty of the composition is that it is malleable, and can be draped over a curved frame while still wet without losing any definition.

To prevent the composition sticking to the mould, first lubricate the latter with a little linseed oil. Flour your hands with some whiting, pick up some of the composition, briefly kneading it with your hands, press it into the mould and smooth it into shape with a knife dipped in hot water. Leave it for five to ten minutes and then carefully lift it out (it will still be soft and flexible). It can now be trimmed to fit the repair and glued into position using rabbit-skin glue* in a proportion of three parts water to one of glue.

It is important to obtain the right thickness of composition for the repair, so mix it carefully. If you make a mistake it is easier to recast the mould than to trim the excess from the back of the impression. Any trimmings of composition can be put back into the pot and re-used.

*FURTHER INFORMATION

Rabbit-skin size, see
  recipe for gesso   page 111

Taking the impression

1 These moulds are made of silicone rubber, backed with plaster for extra rigidity. Before putting composition into the mould it is given a light coating of linseed oil, which helps to release the impression.

2 The composition is put into the mould while it is still warm and flexible. The back is then smoothed with a knife, frequently dipped into hot water to prevent sticking. This action also helps to press the composition into the fine detail of the mould.

3 The composition should still be flexible when it is taken out of the mould so that any excess can be easily trimmed, and if required the ornament can be draped over a contoured frame and glued into place. This is a shallow mould so that the composition is dry enough to lift after a few minutes. Deeper moulds will take longer.

▲ From top to bottom: a frame with a missing cornerpiece which could be cast in composition or plaster. A new composition corner ornament shaped into place. An oval frame with a repair in composition and an ornament modelled in epoxy resin.

MAKING A REPLICA FRAME

One of the most exciting and challenging projects for the picture framer is the construction and decoration of replicas of authentic period frames. The cost of the genuine articles, particularly from the early Renaissance and pre-Renaissance periods, is so prohibitive that only wealthy collectors can afford them.

If you are framing an old picture, or a reproduction of one, you can discover the type of frame that would have been used by conducting some research into the styles of the period. In recent years more attention has been paid to framing old masters in their appropriate frames, and the national collections and even some smaller galleries have begun to buy or reproduce period frames where necessary.

Many of the master pictures in the National Gallery, London, are in their original frames or at least in correct period frames, and there are also catalogues from exhibitions of frames – notably the Metropolitan Museum, New York, and the Art Institute of Chicago. These catalogues contain full details of the frames, with the scale profiles and accurate dimensions which are necessary for authentic replicas. Auction houses often have frame sales, for which well-illustrated catalogues are prepared, but the information is less detailed and not always reliable.

Sometimes a replica frame is made for its own sake rather than as a surround for a picture. The frame can be hung on the wall with nothing in it, or used as a mirror frame. Mirrors can be used in almost any period frame style, allowing the framer to indulge in the extravagant and the ornamental without restraint. A selection of mirror frames can be seen on pages 156-159.

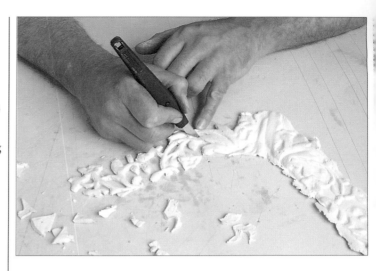

Attaching ornament
1 This corner mould has been taken from a carved 18th-century panel frame. When the composition is taken from the mould it is still wet enough to cut easily. Here the excess composition is being trimmed from the elaborate cut-out corner. The waste pieces of composition can be put back into the pot and re-used.

2 The moulded ornament is glued onto the frame while it is still flexible. A strong mixture of rabbitskin glue (three of water to one of glue) should be used for this. It is usually easier to attach ornament to a frame which has first been gessoed and smoothed.

2 Another piece of board was cut for the back of the frame, and the two pieces were glued and screwed together. The back board creates a rebate for the mirror as well as giving extra strength and depth to the frame.

3 Pastiglia decoration based on 10th-century Iraqui ceramic designs was added to all the sides, and the frame was gilded in white gold over a blue clay ground. The top and bottom backgrounds have been left unburnished, and coated with a weak solution of rabbitskin glue. The frame was made by Aristotelis Zabetas.

Gilded ornament
These two frame corners show a before and after stage, with the one at the top awaiting gilding. The bottom example has been gilded on the patterned design, and the background has been painted green.

Using composite board
1 This replica of a Gothic arched frame has been cut out of medium-density fibre board (MDF). The window aperture and the rounded sight edge were cut and profiled with a router.

CHAPTER 9

A GALLERY OF FRAMES

This chapter is intended as an inspiration to the framemaker, showing the various possibilities that can be explored.

Although there are traditional styles, many of which are still appropriate, there is no one perfect way to frame any picture. Two main factors have to be considered. The frame must suit the picture and enhance our reading of it, but it must also serve a protective function, whether the picture is a work on paper, an oil painting, an embroidery or some other type of image or object. Sometimes, however, the frame can have more importance than the picture. A coloured reproduction, for instance, or a black and white engraving from a pattern book, could become simply one element in a frame which is conceived as a piece of furniture in its own right. This is particularly true of mirror frames; because there is no image, the frame can be made in any style that the maker pleases.

WORKS ON PAPER

Most watercolours, pastels, prints, drawings and photographs need glass to protect them, and a mount or slip frame to separate the glass from the picture and prevent the two from sticking together. The frames are usually light in construction to suit the delicacy of the image.

Watercolours
The delicate, transparent quality of watercolour calls for a discreet framing style. Traditional 19th-century watercolours often had wide neutral margins of mountboard, sometimes with line and wash* decorations harmonizing with colours in the picture. Thin gilt frames with small floral ornaments were popular, among other styles, and added a restrained richness to the subdued tones of the watercolour.

Modern watercolours are often brighter and more vibrant than their predecessors, and call for a bolder display. Colour washes* over the frame can be attractive, and can be used to echo colours in the picture. Natural and coloured wood, as well as more contemporary finishes such as bright enamels and metallic frames, are widely used, as are coloured mounts.

◄ The simple shape and warm tones of this natural wood frame work well with the strong 19th-century watercolour by Peter de Wint. A more complex treatment, or a decorated or coloured mount, could have lessened its impact.

◄ Ray Willingham has framed his own watercolour with a discreet natural-wood moulding, which contrasts nicely with the pale green of the mount. The mount has a white inner border with a gold pen line separating the two colours.

▶ Adèle Seigal's watercolour is strong enough to benefit from an unusual treatment – a distressed gilt frame and no mount. The gold leaf has been distressed most heavily at the sight edge, where the visible underlayer of red burnishing clay echoes the warm red-browns in the painting. The frame was made by Harry Seigal.

◀ A backmounting method has been used here, with the picture fixed to one piece of mountboard and the main window mount cut from another. This gives an effect similar to that of a floating frame (see page 49), where the edges of the picture are not hidden by a rebate or the edges of the mount. The treatment gives additional importance to the small image, further enhanced by the wide reverse bevel gilt moulding. The painting is by Andrew Hewkin and the frame by James Frames (James Sullivan).

There is an ever-increasing range of coloured mountcard, in both vivid and subdued colours, which can be used to complement both the frame and the picture.

Pastels

Pastels, being an older medium than watercolour, have a longer tradition of framing. The richness of the chalk colours is closer to oil painting than to watercolour, and can stand a bolder framed display. Traditionally pastels were framed in similar surrounds to oil paintings, though the mouldings were usually thinner. They were glazed and separated from the glass by concealed blocks of wood. No mounts were used, although sometimes decorated slip frames performed the same function.

Unlike watercolours, pastels do not fade with time, but they are extremely vulnerable to surface damage, and need the protection of a well-made frame. Many pastellists fix their work before framing, but others do not, as fixative has a darkening effect on the colours. Even when fixed, the soft pigment can easily smudge and fall off the paper surface. These days pastels are usually framed like watercolours, with mounts and a similar style of moulding. This suits some delicate works, but a more dramatic presentation can be tried for the stronger styles.

Prints

The traditional print frame was even more reserved than the period watercolour frame. Etchings and engravings had ivory or pale grey mounts lightly decorated with pen and

▲ This strong and colourful pastel painting called for an equally positive framing treatment. The frame was hand-coloured by Adèle Seigal with gouache paints, and given a brilliant red sight edge which both picks up colours in the painting and separates the frame from the dark blue mount.

◄ The warmth of the terracotta and gold in this distressed gilt frame combines well with this engraving, the sepia tones of a Leonardo drawing.

wash lines. The frame was often thin flat wood, gessoed and black-lacquered. This sombre style of frame is less favoured now, but it suits monochrome prints very well, as does the "Hogarth" style frame, a variation of the same type, but with small gilt beadings either side of the black moulding.

Bolder contemporary prints need a more solid approach. Wider natural-wood frames are frequently used, and so are coloured mouldings and mountboard. Smaller prints can be enhanced by using wide mounts, which has the effect of focusing attention on a small image.

Maps and documents

These have traditionally been framed in natural wood. At the turn of this century there was a fashion for bird's-eye maple veneer and other exotic woods, with gold or silver slips. The subtle colours of the wood add a little warmth to the subdued colouring.

Where the edge of the paper or parchment is a feature, the map or document can be mounted onto a backing card with another window mount on top to expose the edges. This practice is also frequently followed with prints, particularly etchings, where the paper, often hand made, is an essential element of the overall image.

Photographs

Old photographs usually look best in a frame of the same period, which is often similar to a watercolour frame, with a neutral-coloured window mount and a thin moulding. *Intimate family photographs of past generations in soft sepia*

▷ 148

▲ The narrow black-lacquered frame and minimal mount provide the perfect setting for this powerful print by Tsugumi Ota. A window mount has not been used, as the irregular edges of the paper form an integral part of the image. Frame by John Jones Frames.

▲ This strong woodblock print by Julian Meredith lent itself to a similar pattern on the frame, which is made of ash, scorched to deepen the grain and then limed (see page 74) for greater contrast. The frame is by Robert Cunning.

◄ An etching of children in the west of Ireland by Gerard Brockhurst has been framed in the traditional manner for prints, namely a thin black lacquer frame with a neutral off-white mount.

▲ A "Hogarth" style frame, made of oak with a gilt ball ornament on the sight edge. has been used for this decorative woodblock print of a pineapple. The warm colours of the print and the frame are offset by the cool blue of the mount. Both the etching anc the frame are by Derek James.

▲ This lively watercolour by Rowlandson has a thin natural-wood frame that is lighter in colour on the outer edge, with a thin line of gold on the sight edge. The double mount is decorated with pale wash lines on the inside, which complement the delicate shading in the picture.

tones are often given fabric frames of velvet or leather. These might be frames for a desk or table top, with a strut back, similarly covered in fabric.

Contemporary photographs, particularly "art photographs", are most commonly framed in an austere manner. Black and white photographs cannot usually stand much colour on the frame, and thin black frames are used a lot for modern displays of both colour and black and white prints. This is a safe if unadventurous way to frame photographs. Natural wood, sometimes limed, adds a restrained colour which is suitable for the stark quality of many contemporary photographs.

At a recent exhibition of "master" photographers of the 1920s and 1930s at the Hayward Gallery in London, wide silver gilt frames, distressed* to show a black clay undercoat, were used very effectively. This was a more dramatic style of framing, but the cool silver on black repeated the black and white of the photograph in a different key.

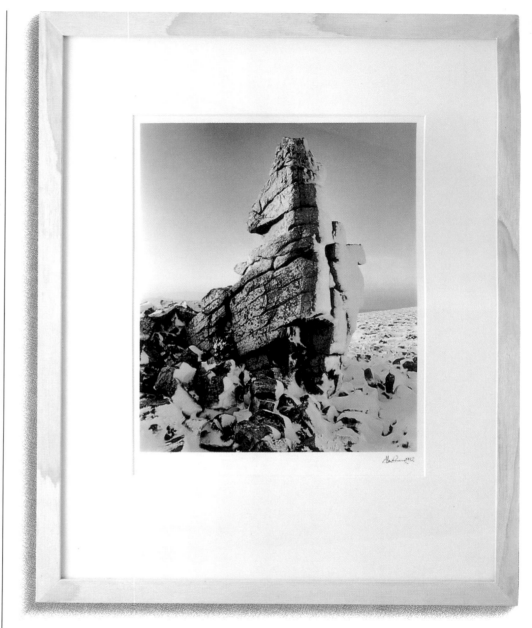

▲ This highly dramatic black and white photograph by Alex Ramsey needs a restrained presentation. The simple flat shape and restrained colour of the limed ash frame complement the image without interfering with our perception.

▶ An image like this photograph by Andy Goldsworthy, with its brilliant colours and wealth of detail, needs as little competition from the frame as possible. The plain, wide mount and narrow white square-sectioned moulding provide an elegant but unobtrusive setting. Frame by John Jones Frames.

OILS AND ACRYLICS

Most oil and acrylic paintings are done on canvases (canvas stretched over a framework of wooden slats) or boards. Paintings on boards or panels present no problems for the framemaker, but canvases can become slightly distorted, and the overlap of canvas is thicker at the corners, so you will have to allow for these discrepancies as well as making sure that the rebate of the moulding is deep enough to accommodate the wooden stretchers.

Oil and acrylics are more robust and less prone to damage than works on paper, and thus do not usually need glass to protect them. Although most of the oil paintings you will see in a major art gallery do have glass, nowadays the majority are framed without it so that the texture of the paint surface is more readily appreciated. Mounts are not used, and the mouldings are usually wider than those traditionally used for works on paper.

There are exceptions to this rule. Small paintings done on thin board, with a fairly flat and unobtrusive paint surface, can benefit from being framed very much like watercolours, that is, glazed and mounted. A painting treated like this is shown on page 154.

◀ The pale greys of the sky and water are an important feature in this painting by Peter Graham, and the frame has been painted to echo them, with a slightly warmer beige-grey on the inner slip frame. The width of the moulding gives the frame an imposing presence, while the pale colour prevents it from dominating the picture. Frame by Art Works The Framemakers (Stephen Carruthers).

◀ The warm earth colours in this sunny landscape have been repeated in the terre verte (green) central border of burnished clay, and in the outer gilt edge which has been distressed to reveal the terracotta beneath. The frame and painting are by Ludmilla Thurlow.

▲ Very small paintings – this one is only about 20cm (8 in) across – often benefit from a wide, ornate frame. The painting is by David Warilow and the frame by John Jones Frames.

In general, small paintings look best in wide frames, which gives them additional presence, while large, bold paintings can often more or less stand by themselves, with a minimal frame or, in the case of pictures on canvas, a plain wood batten nailed round the edges. A floating frame*, in which the edges of the picture are not hidden by a rebate can look very effective, as this has the effect of thrusting the picture forward.

Apart from these general guidelines, there are no hard and fast rules, and over the centuries many different styles of frame have been used, ranging from the elaborate architectural motifs seen on frames of the Renaissance period, through carved, moulded and lavishly gilded frames to the more restrained natural wood or subtly decorated frames of the present time.

✱FURTHER INFORMATION

Floating frames   page 49

◀ At first sight the frame seems very distinct from the picture, but there is a relationship, as the elaborate burnished black and silver frame has panels illustrating biblical stories. The central theme of the painting is the Flight to Egypt. The painting and frame are by Rosemary Williams.

▼ A floating frame allows the complete painting to be seen, as the edges are not covered by a rebate. This painting by Adèle Seigal is on canvas, which stands proud of the dark grey inner frame. The frame was made by Harry Seigal.

◄ Unusually, this painting has been given a cabinet-style frame with glass. The artist, George Rowlett, paints in thick impastos, building up almost three-dimensional effects, so this treatment is highly suitable both from an aesthetic and a practical point of view – the peaks and crevices of thick paint collect dirt very quickly. Frame by John Jones Frames.

◄ This wide, gently curving reverse moulding with no ornamentation sets off the painting very well. The starkness of the painted finish is relieved by a slight texture, and the inner slip provides a touch of warm colour. The painting is by Peter Graham and the frame by Art Works, The Framemakers (Stephen Carruthers).

◀ Although the frame is older than the picture, which is a late Impressionist-style work, it combines well with this 19th-century moulded frame. The pattern of the frame was softened with white colour to subdue the gilt, little of which now remains.

▶ Small oil paintings can look rather lost when hung on the wall. One solution is to use a wide, ornate frame, as in the example on page 151. Another is to treat them in a similar way to a watercolour, with a mount and glass. For works painted on thin card, as this one is, the method is also practical, as the glass gives protection. The painting is by Jeremy Galton and the frame by Highgate Framers.

▶ Again the Impressionist style painting is displayed to advantage in a period frame. A few gilded highlights remain of the original gold pattern which helps to lighten the frame colour.

MIRROR FRAMES

Unlike other frames, those for mirrors have no competition – there is no picture to enhance, complement or contrast with the frame. For this reason the tradition of mirror frames is different to that of picture frames, owing more to the world of interior design. Some of the most inventive and beautiful mirror frames have been, and still are, made or designed by furniture makers. There are many historical examples of mirror frames, from the large carved pier glasses of the Rococo period to the more solid oak and mahogany hall mirrors of Victorian times.

Because the frames are made for their own sake, they can be as elaborate as you like in shape and design, with any paint finish or gilding effect you feel inclined to try out. If you are making a frame for a specific room, you will of course have to consider the existing decor, but otherwise there are no constraints.

One practical point to bear in mind is that a mirror will reflect the inside rebate of the frame, so this must be painted (or gilded) in the same way as the rest of the frame. Otherwise the natural colour of the wood will show and detract from the overall effect.

▲ These highly ornate mirror frames with a carved and gilded imperial eagle on top were made in the Empire period in about 1820. The imperial taste was imported from France to England and the frames were made in both countries at the beginning of the 19th century.

► A small dressing-table mirror frame has been made with imitation tortoiseshell (see page 124) laid onto a silver ground so that light is reflected through the shell. Black lacquer on either side gives a dramatic edge to the frame.

▼ The cassetta style, with a flat central section, lends itself to decoration, and here has been finely engraved (see page 126) with an arabic design. The gold has been distressed and coloured for a mature appearance. Frame made by Aritotelis Zabetas.

▼ The extended corner (see page 42) featured here is a popular motif for mirror frames. The elaborate moulded decoration around the frame has an Art Nouveau design on a "woven" background.

▲ The Neoclassical pillars at the side of this early 19th-century overmantel mirror are carried onto the top of the frame as well. The black reeded inner frame is repeated at the base of the frame.

◀ Antique picture frames are often used for mirrors, and this 19th-century moulded frame with corner leaf and centre ornaments is eminently suitable.

► This square flat mirror frame has punched, painted and sgraffito decorations (see pages 125 and 126) on a gold ground. The mirror has been made by laying silver leaf onto glass, giving an antique appearance. Frame and mirror by Rosemary Williams.

▼ A cassetta-style mirror frame with a sgraffito border of black over gold. The outer and sight edges are in bright burnished gold, and the mirror has been hand silvered. Frame and mirror made by Michele Riley.

▲ This is part of a large oval frame with a running pattern of flowers and leaves. It has been gilded with imitation gold, and patinated using brown colour, particularly in the recesses of the ornament.

TEXTILES AND OBJECTS

Textiles, whether woven or embroidered, have different physical characteristics from paintings, and some consideration needs to be given to this. Embroideries are sometimes framed without glass so that their texture can be seen and appreciated, but this does, of course, make them vulnerable to dirt and atmospheric conditions.

The majority of textiles, particularly valuable ones, are mounted and glazed to protect them. Frames can vary from thin, unobtrusive mouldings to decorated ones using colours that complement or contrast with those in the textile. The mounting of textiles can present a problem, as the conventional matt-surface coloured mountboard does not always make a suitable border. Fabric mounts* can look effective, or double mounts* with a gilded or contrast-coloured inner border.

Textiles can also be framed without mounts, treated rather like an oil painting, but with glass. This can be effective for bold, colourful embroideries or heavily textured ones such as canvas work. It is important that the glass does not touch the embroidery, so a slip frame* or some form of insert is often used below the glass.

◄ These two crewel work embroideries based on Jacobean designs are intended to be hung as a pair, and are framed almost identically, the only difference being in the mounts. These are decorated with strands of the wool used in the embroideries, oranges and yellows in one case and red in the other. Holes were pierced at the corners of the mount and the wool was pulled taut at the back, forming decorative textured lines of colour. Embroideries and frames are by Barbara Skelt.

► This contemporary embroidery has been double-mounted behind glass, and the blue colour in the mount is repeated in the frame. The flat edge of the frame has been covered with veneer and the central margin is gilded, a decorative style which complements this richly textured embroidery. The embroidery is by Bobby Britnell and the frame by Isabella Kocum.

Small objects – medals, jewellery, fans, feathers and so on – and more three-dimensional type of embroidery, such as stumpwork, where some of the shapes are padded – will need cabinet or box frames*. These not only provide sufficient depth to house the objects; they also enhance the presentation.

Most moulding suppliers stock a variety of deep mouldings for box frames, and standard moulding profiles can be adapted by adding a further section of wood to the bottom. For simple displays, for example, a half- or quarter-round section can be added to the top of a section of wood 7.5×2.5 cm (3×1 inch) to make an effective deep frame. If glass is used, it must be held at the front of the frame, either using visible inner frames or invisible small blocks. The inside edges of the frame will be seen, so they must be taken into account in the overall decorative scheme.

＊FURTHER INFORMATION

Fabric mounts   page 66
Double and treble
   mounts   page 56
Slips and box frames   page 46

◀ This unusual object is a painting of a steamship on a leaf. It has been back-mounted onto black velvet, and has a simple natural-wood frame which traps the glass at the front as in a cabinet.

◀ This reverse appliqué design by Bobby Britnell has a repeating pattern which is echoed in the textured linear decoration of the frame. The pinks and purples in the textile have been picked up on the frame and highlighted with silver wax. The method used for texturing and painting the frame is shown on pages 84-85.

▶ This highly decorative embroidery with silver and gold stitching and elaborate floral margins needs a simple presentation. The natural wood frame has been limed (see page 74) and the mount is a warm cream which sets off the rich colouring of the embroidery.

CLASSIC FRAMES

The development of picture framing is inextricably linked to that of architecture and furniture making, and when tastes in interior design changed and evolved, so did the design of frames. Paintings of earlier periods were often reframed in the prevailing taste of the time, and in national collections until quite recently one could see 15th- and 16th-century Italian paintings in 18th- and 19th-century French and Northern European frames, reflecting the collector's taste rather than the period design. This was not considered odd or inappropriate, but recently more attention has been given to acquiring or reproducing the correct period frame for a particular picture. Along with this change has come a new appreciation of the artistry of the picture framer, and exhibitions of classic period frames are held.

Pre-Renaissance paintings were usually integral with their frames. The painting was done on the central part of a panel, which was cut out and planed so that a hollow area was formed. The surrounding bevel and ridge were often gilded and decorated. As paintings became more monumental, panels were joined together to form larger painted areas (canvas over stretchers was later used), and simple mouldings were made to be attached to the panels.

Separated frames began to be made for the first time during the Renaissance, when tools and carpentry techniques became more sophisticated and the output of paintings increased dramatically. This was the great period of framemaking, and Renaissance designs still form the basis of many frames used today.

Italian design was copied and modified by the French and Spanish and the Northern European countries, and many distinctive styles evolved. The French made elaborately carved swept-shaped frames, elegantly designed and richly gilded. Spanish frames were often darkly coloured with heavily carved corner and centre ornaments in gold. The Netherlands and the Protestant countries of Northern Europe tended towards a more austere style, with dark, heavy woods such as ebony and walnut carved in flutes and reeds with only small amounts of gold. These different cultures produced distinctive "classic" period frames which since the 19th century have been further copied and embellished. They are also often reproduced using moulded rather than carved forms.

▲ These grand French Neoclassical frames of the 18th and 19th centuries have distinctive top ornaments, carved and modelled, with elaborate ribbons and wreaths. The top-heavy appearance is particularly suitable for mirrors and some portraits.

▶ A very lavish and richly carved frame surrounds this portrait of Queen Anne. The frame was made in England, and the dense and intricate carving is reminiscent of the great English woodcarver of the same period, Grinling Gibbons.

▲ These lovely Italian frames of the 17th and 18th centuries refer back to the designs and patterns of the Renaissance. They are richly decorated with sgraffito, engraved and punched patterns, and have borders of carved foliage.

UNUSUAL FRAMES

The most widely used shapes for frames, for obvious reasons, are rectangles and squares, though ovals and circles* are now becoming increasingly popular, as are hexagonal and octagonal frames*. The latter are no more difficult to make than rectangular frames, as most mitre saws can be adjusted to the correct angle for the corners. Mount cutters* which will cut circles and ovals are now available, though the frames themselves are trickier to make.

Sometimes an image seems to call for a more unusual display, a famous example being the painting of a female nude by the Surrealist painter René Magritte, in which the wooden frame bends to follow the contours of the body. Another well-known Surrealist, Giorgio de Chirico, painted a triangular picture, which was naturally set in a triangular frame. Even when the image itself is a normal shape, an irregular-shaped frame can make an eye-catching wall display, and some craftsmen like to produce unusual frames for their own sake, particularly for mirrors, where there is no image to dictate the shape.

▲ This pedimented frame was made before the painting was done, and suggested the classical theme of the picture. The whole frame has been marbled (see page 96) and the pillars have been marbled in a different colour and gilded. The painting and frame are by Robert Cunning.

✱FURTHER INFORMATION

Pentagons, hexagons and
   octagons   page 50
Mountcutters   page 16
Eggshell inlay   page 95

◀ John Anderson began by making frames for his own paintings, but gradually the frames actually became the paintings. He likes painting on wood or veneer, and achieves background colours with spirit-soluble dyes mixed with shellac, built up and burnished after each coat. For details, he uses acrylic, and he often includes touches of inlay, such as the bird in this example.

▲ The dramatic jagged and angular nature of the print has been carried through in an ingenious way onto the mount and frame. The frame is made with cut-outs and appliqué wood sections. Frame and print are both by Ray Willingham.

► The flat border frame for this colourful pastel has been decorated by the artist, Frances Treanor, in a similar style, and provides an intriguing extension of the painting.

► This unusual frame is decorated with eggshells, and grouted so that it has the appearance of a mosaic. The oriental nature of the painting suggested this traditional Japanese technique, which is demonstrated on page 95. The painting and frame are by Derek James.

Triptych frames were initially conceived to transport elaborate altarpieces safely. The plain external doors protected the rich internal paintings and frames inside. Here, although there are paintings on the outer doors also, the idea has been retained by gilding the inner frame only. The doors have double rebates to house the panels, and are hinged on the outside of the central frame. The paintings and frame are by Robert Cunning.

▲ This "frame within a frame" has a small gilt inner surround attached to a backing card. The whole is glazed and contained within a traditional-style Dutch reeded frame. The painting is by Andrew Hewkin and the frame by James Frames (James Sullivan).

DISPLAYING PICTURES

There are no hard and fast rules about just where and how you should hang your picture frames; the best rule of thumb is whether or not you like the finished results. However, there are guidelines you can follow regarding the grouping and arrangement.

Most pictures look best hung in groups to form a block rather than spaced out randomly over a large area. Unless a picture is fairly large it's best not to hang it alone on the wall or it can look lost. The only exceptions are very large posters, prints or ornate frames which are visually strong and imposing enough to make a statement by themselves.

Before you start to hammer picture-pins in the wall, experiment with the layout by laying the framed images in groups on the floor. This will enable you to play around with sizes, shapes and colours until you find a grouping you like. To work out the arrangement precisely, you can measure the wall space available and then mark out these boundaries on the floor with lengths of string.

Choosing the wall
Groups of pictures look best integrated as closely as possible with furnishings or any architectural features in a room. Use furniture as a guide for the outer vertical boundaries of your group. These might align with a sideboard or chest of drawers, for instance, in which case you can imagine a rectangle drawn upwards on the wall from the edges of the piece of furniture. This same principle works for the space above a bed or behind a settee.

The way your walls are decorated will dictate which pictures look best on them. White or plain light-coloured walls look best with clear strong colours and pictures displayed in simple frames without mounts. Monochrome prints and photos also look very effective on light walls. For coloured walls, it's a good idea to either echo the colour scheme of the room in the picture mount or use the mount as an effective contrast. If walls are painted in plain dark colours, the pictures may need light-coloured mounts.

Patterned walls need the most care, as the picture and the wallcovering should not seem to be jostling with each other for attention. The colouring, size and style of the wallcovering pattern will dictate the type of frame that looks best, but some sort of mount is almost always essential to give the picture clear definition.

Practicalities
While just about any flat vertical surface can become home to a picture frame, try not to hang pictures where they will be constantly knocked – in a narrow hallway or close to the back of a chair – or you will be constantly having to straighten them.

▼ The narrow space between the windows is accentuated with a pair of matching prints in identical frames. Positioned above a side table, they draw the eye down towards the bowl of flowers and the table display.

Avoid hanging pictures above a radiator, as the rising heat, together with dust and grease carried upwards, can damage the picture and may crack the glue of the frame. In general, pictures should not be hung in direct sunlight or opposite a window, especially if they are valuable. Watercolours are particularly vulnerable, as they fade easily, apart from which, if the picture is glazed the reflection of the window can make it difficult to see the image.

Building a shape
If you have traditional picture rails you can use picture hooks to support large frames hung on two chains – one at each

corner of the top of the frame. Repeat this idea around the room – the best effect comes from keeping the tops of all the pictures at the same height.

A group of pictures will look best if it does not appear to split obviously into either half or quarters. Groups that fall naturally into thirds tend to be more harmonious. Hang the central picture – the most eye-catching and interesting – at eye-level. This can either be your eye-level when standing or when seated; the latter could be effective in a dining room, for instance. As a rule, larger pictures look best when placed at the bottom of a group, otherwise the arrangement can look top heavy.

There are two basic types of grouping: geometric and informal. For the former, the pictures can be hung in a straight line or arranged in a neat square or rectangle. Formal geometric groups work best when the frame mouldings are identical and the pictures the same shape and size. This style works well with modern furnishings, and is a good way to display a set of matching prints or photographs.

A geometric picture arrangement can be used either to emphasize or to play down the proportions of a room. A long horizontal line of pictures will have the effect of lessening the height of a tall, lofty ceiling, while a tall column of pictures takes the eye upwards and makes a room with a low ceiling seem taller and more spacious.

For pictures of different sizes, shapes and types, you will need an informal arrangement. Be prepared to experiment to find the most pleasing distribution of shapes – it may help to imagine the outline of the group forming a rectangle, circle or triangle. Generally, large pictures look best with fairly wide gaps between them, while smaller pictures need to be hung closer together to avoid a sparse appearance.

Lighting
Not all pictures look their best when strongly lit. You may wish to highlight the central frame in a group or highlight just one or two smaller frames. Apart from natural daylight, there are basically two ways to light pictures: either by spotlighting (positioning an ordinary light or spotlight to shine onto the picture from somewhere in the room) or by fixing a light on or near the frame itself. Experiment using the types of lamp mentioned below until you find exactly the effect you want.

Uplighters give an even, diffused light. They can be positioned on a table, on the floor directly under the frames, or hidden among foliage or behind a chair. Spotlights can be adjusted to create direct or reflected light. Low-voltage tungsten-halogen spotlights are small and discreet and can be used as ceiling lights, as individual wall-spots, in a standard-style floor fitting, or two or more individual spots can be mounted on a strip track attached to the wall or ceiling.

A fluorescent strip will light a complete group of pictures. A good technique to use in a large room is to fit a diffuser to angle the light onto the pictures and choose a

"daylight" coloured lamp for the most natural effect.

Picture lamps are individual lights attached directly to the picture or to the wall just above it. They are available in a range of modern and traditional styles, so can be chosen to match both your room and the picture. Make sure the fitting is wide enough to light the whole picture – it should be about two thirds of the picture's width. If it throws a reflection on the glass or varnish you can effectively reduce it simply by tilting the picture slightly towards the floor.

▲ An eclectic mixture of frames in different sizes, shapes and with very different images fills one complete wall. Careful positioning of frames keeps the balance correct between large and small-sized frames. With a plain dark background of cork tiles, each picture needs either a contrasting frame or a coloured mount to help it stand out. The single picture on the right is large enough – and with a strong image – to make a statement all on its own.

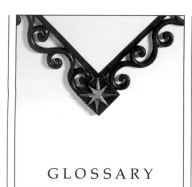

GLOSSARY

Aniline dyes
Synthetic dyes originally made from aniline, a colourless, oily liquid. The dyes are bought in powdered form, and can be mixed with methylated spirits to make wood dyes, or with **Shellac** to make coloured lacquers and varnishes.

Beading
Narrow strip of wood, often ornamental, sometimes used as an additional component of a frame.

Beeswax
Natural wax made from honeycombs, used on its own as a polish or as a base for coloured polishes and imitation golds (*see* **Bronze powders**).

Bevel
The sloping edge on the inside window of a **Mount**; the sloping edge of a ruler or straight-edge used for cutting bevels.

Biscuit joiner
A miniature saw that cuts grooves across the backs of mitre joints into which a wedge of wood is inserted to strengthen them.

Bole *see* **Burnishing clay**

Box frames
Deep frames designed to display three-dimensional objects such as medals behind glass. Also used for embroideries and sometimes for oil paintings with a particularly thick build-up of paint. Sometimes called cabinet frames.

Bronze powder
Finely powdered base metals, usually bronze, used to make imitation gold and gold paint.

Burnishers
Tools used in the water-gilding method to rub the gold or silver leaf to a smooth, shiny finish. The traditional burnishers have smooth, curved ends made of agate, set in plain wooden handles.

Burnishing clay
Fine clay coloured with pigment, used in the preparation of surfaces for gilding. The traditional colour used under gold leaf is a dark terracotta, but the clay is available in a number of different colours. It can be bought as a paste or in a solid cone.

Button polish *see under* **Shellac**

Cabinet frames *see* **Box frames**

Carnauba wax
Wax obtained from the leaves of the Brazilian fan-palm tree, used with beeswax in the preparation of gold and silver waxes.

Carragheen moss
Type of seaweed used in combination with special inks for marbling paper.

Casein
Strongly adhesive substance made from the curd of milk. Used as a binder for paints and as a glue. A form of **Gesso** can be made using casein as an alternative to **Rabbit-skin glue**.

Cassetta frame
A traditional type of frame which has a border within an outer moulding. The borders are often richly decorated.

Conservation board
Mountboard made from rag or woodpulp specially treated to remove acids, which can be harmful to valuable works on paper.

Craquelure
The fine cracks often seen on old oil paintings. The effect is sometimes deliberately induced on frames by putting a fast-drying paint or varnish over a slow-drying one.

Decoupage
Form of decoration in which pieces of cut paper are glued onto the frame moulding and then treated with successive layers of varnish. The paper used can be plain coloured paper, photographic or other images from magazines, or photostats, either coloured or black and white.

Distressing
Method of simulating the patina of age on a frame by rubbing away some of the top layer of gilt or paint so that the base colour shows through.

Epoxy resins
Chemically synthesized resin glues, usually in two parts, the glue itself and a hardener. Some epoxy resins are bought in powder form, with the hardener incorporated, and are mixed with water.

Floating frame
A frame designed so that the picture does not fit behind a rebate, but is either proud of its border or flush with it. Floating frames are mainly used for oil or acrylic paintings on panels, where the image extends fully to the edges.

Foxing
The brown spots of mildew often seen on old mounts, prints or watercolours, caused by damp.

French polish *see under* **Shellac**

Fuming
Colouring wood by exposing it to the fumes of ammonia.

Gesso
Brilliant white preparation made from whiting (chalk) and **Rabbit-skin glue** size or **Casein** size, used to prepare surfaces for gilding before the application of **Burnishing clay**. Acrylic gesso, bought ready made, is produced principally as a ground for paintings, and is less suitable for preparing wood surfaces, as it cannot be sanded to such a smooth surface.

Gilt
The term covering all water-gilded or transfer-gilded surfaces, whether gold or silver. *See also* **Gold leaf, Transfer gilding, Water gilding**.

Glazing
The word has two meanings. 1: to cover a picture with glass; 2: to apply a thin, transparent layer of colour over another colour.

Glazing gun
A type of stapler which shoots flat, triangular-section tacks into the back of the frame.

Gold leaf
Thin sheets of beaten gold (or silver) applied over a surface prepared with **Gesso** and **Burnishing clay**. The leaf used in **Transfer gilding** has a paper backing.

Gold size
A viscous glue substance traditionally used in **Transfer gilding** to secure the gold or silver leaf to the prepared surface. A water-soluble glue has now been developed as an alternative.

Graining
Simulating the grain of wood with paints and glazes applied over an undercoat. An inexpensive wood can be treated in this way to resemble a rare and exotic one.

Lacquer
A hard, glossy paint made with cellulose derivatives or by dissolving pigments or aniline dyes in **Shellac**.

Liming
Treating raw wood by pushing white pigment into the grain. Oak and ash are the woods most commonly limed.

Mitre
The 45° angled cut made in each end of a piece of frame moulding so that they meet at a 90° angle (mitre joint).

Mitre saw
A saw designed specifically for cutting mitres. The blade is held in place by two steel columns mounted on a metal base.

Moulding
A shaped length of wood. Picture-frame mouldings have a **Rebate** behind which the picture fits (and the mount and glass if used). Carpenter's mouldings, used for skirting-boards, trimmings around doors etc., have no rebate, but can sometimes be adapted for framemaking.

Mount
The card surround used to protect and display a work on paper. Mounts are usually cut with a window, behind which the picture fits, and the inner edges are bevelled.

Pastiglia
An extra-thick **Gesso** used for ornamental work on frames. Patterns are built up in relief and then gilded.

Pearl glue
Animal-skin glue obtained as granules, which are mixed with water and heated before use. This was the traditional glue for woodworking before the advent of the various synthetic glues.

Polyurethane varnish
Frequently used instead of French polish (*see under* **Shellac**) to finish and protect natural wood. It is available in gloss and matt finishes, and is tough and durable. However, it tends to discolour with time.

Profile
The word used to describe the shape of a **Moulding**.

PVA
Polyvinyl acetate, a synthetic resin glue in the form of a thick white liquid. Now the glue most commonly used in framemaking and other woodworking. PVA, in a diluted form, is also used as a paint medium.

Ox gall
A medium used in the manufacture of watercolours and also sometimes as a paint medium. It breaks the tension of the water and makes the paint flow more freely.

Rabbit-skin glue
Bought in granules and mixed and heated to make glue or **Size**. This is used for treating raw wood, to make it less absorbent, and in the preparation of **Gesso**. (*See also* **Casein**.)

Rag rolling
Method of decorating wood by laying down paint and pushing a rag in various directions along it to produce a textured effect.

Rebate
The L-shaped groove on the inside edge of a picture-frame moulding into which the picture, glass, mount and backing board fit. Sometimes called rabbet.

Reverse moulding
A moulding which has the highest part next to the picture, and slopes away at the outer edge.

Router
A machine used by professional framemakers for cutting moulding shapes, grooves and rebates.

Sgraffito
A method of decoration in which fine lines and patterns are scratched into a top layer of paint or gilt, leaving the colour beneath showing through.

Shellac
A varnish made from the resin secreted by the lac insect, suspended in alcohol. It is variously coloured from pale yellow to dark brown, and is known by a number of different names, including French polish, button polish and garnet polish. It can also be mixed with **Aniline dyes**. Shellac seals the grain and protects the wood, but is neither heat- nor spirit-resistant.

Sight edge
The inner edge of the frame moulding, next to the picture.

Size
A weak solution of glue used to seal wood and reduce its absorbency before painting, and as an ingredient in the preparation of **Gesso**. (*See also* **Casein** and **Rabbit-skin glue**.)

Slip frame
A flat, narrow strip of wood, sometimes gilded or decorated, inserted between the main frame and the picture. Slips are often used to protect the picture by providing more space between it and the glass, but they can also be purely decorative.

Spattering
Decorating a surface by flicking droplets of paint over it. Spattering can achieve subtle and complex effects of colour, and can be used for both frames and mounts.

Sponging
Creating textured effects by applying paint with a sponge, or laying a coat of paint and then dabbing into it. This method can also be used for both frames and mounts.

Tabernacle frame
A traditional type of frame which has a decorative panel or pediment fitted to the top. Now used more frequently for mirrors than for pictures.

Three-dimensional frame *see* **Box frame**.

Transfer gilding
Method of gilding in which glue is used to fasten the leaf to the prepared surface. The leaf usually has a paper backing, which is peeled off once the gilt is in place. The process is faster and easier than **Water gilding**, but transfer leaf cannot be burnished.

Trimmer
A tool used for trimming the end-grain of wood, for both **Mitres** and 90° cuts.

Underpinner
A machine used by professional framemakers to join the frame by shooting metal wedges into the back of the mitre joint. Hand-operated underpinners are now becoming available.

Veneer
Thin sheets of wood which can be bonded to the surface of a less expensive wood. Some of the rarer and more exotic woods are only available as veneers.

Wash line
A form of decoration used on mounts, usually for watercolours or old prints. A pale wash of watercolour is painted around the whole mount a small distance from the window aperture, and finished with fine pen lines.

Water gilding
The traditional method of gilding, in which loose gold or silver leaf is applied on a surface prepared with **Gesso** and **Burnishing clay**. No glue is used.

Whiting
A fine chalk which together with **Rabbit-skin glue size**, is the principal ingredient of **Gesso**. The best is called gilder's whiting.

INDEX

Page numbers in *italic* refer to the illustrations

CREDITS

The author and publishers would like to thank all those who made their frames available for photography. Wherever possible, the makers of frames are credited in the captions to the illustrations, but we would also like to thank those who kindly loaned frames, equipment or photographs, but whose names do not appear in the book. **Mary Alliston LMPA,** page 73; **Faber Blinds** pages 170, 171; **J. Fisher and Son,** page 18; **Franchis Locks and Tools,** pages 14-15; **Bryant Jackson**

Communications (Arquati mouldings), pages 21, 119; **Lapis,** page 151; **Cathy Meeus,** pages 142, 146 bottom, 147, 145 top, 155; **Paul Mitchell Antiques Ltd,** pages 164-5; **Now and Then,** pages 148-9, 156-7; **Origin Framing Supplies,** pages 13, 16-17, 21, 58, 77; **Paperchase,** pages 61, 62; **Porter Design,** page 140; **Dr and Mrs Wynne Williams,** page 162 top.

The author offers particular thanks to the following for their invaluable help in the preparation of this book. **Isabella Kocum** for gilding and decorating frames; **John Spencer** for making and decorating mounts; **Louise Taylor** for her demonstration of wood graining; **Derek James, Martin Britnell** and **Alistair MacDonald** for making frames, and **Jana Valencic** for general organization and administration.